FORGET THE PHARMACY-
GROW YOUR OWN MEDICINE

FORGET THE PHARMACY-GROW YOUR OWN MEDICINE

The Homesteader's Ultimate Self-Sufficient Guide To Grow Herbs, Craft Natural Remedies, And Treat Common Health, First Aid, And Illnesses Proactively

JENNI REMPEL

CONTENTS

Section Three

Section Five

For My Da••y, Duncan Watson, who is an amazing •a•. He showe• up for my soccer practices, ball games, boring high school, college, an• university gra•uations, an• every other significant life event. He took my sister & me camping, taught us how to renovate houses, an• took us on worl• vacations. He is a wise, clever, an• goo• man. He loves me. An• he's a great gar•ener. I wish I ha• listene• more when I was a ki• because he grows a mean Kale, even though my mom, Maire, hates it!

Although this man struggles now with Parkinson's Disease, an• things are more challenging than they use• to be, very har• in fact, nothing •iminishes his greatness to me.

To my Da•, my first love, who has always tol• me how much he loves me.

An• I love you too, Da•.

DOWNLOAD YOUR FREE FULL COLOR REFERENCE CHART OF EVERY HERB IN THIS BOOK

Each herb has a full color picture as well as a list of the benefits we reviewed. You can print this handy guide as a quick reference.

To download your FREE "Forget the Pharmacy – Grow Your Own Medicine Reference Chart", scan this QR code

or go to

referenceguide.homesteadmindset.com

Thank you for rea•ing this book an• your won•erful support. I wish you every blessing an• goo• health! Jenni

OTHER BOOKS BY JENNI REMPEL

FORGET THE PHARMACY - GROW YOUR OWN MEDICINE

THE COMPREHENSIVE HERBAL HANDBOOK (2 IN 1)

THE HERBALIST'S HEALING GARDEN FOR BEGINNERS

THE HOMESTEADER HERBAL HANDBOOK

SPANISH

EL-MANUAL-COMPLETO-DE-HIERBAS-MEDICINALES (2 EN 1)

EL MANUAL DE HIERBAS DEL HORTELANO

OLVIDATE DE LA FARMACIA – CULTIVA TU PROPIA MEDICINA

GERMAN

VERGESSEN SIE DIE APOTHEKE – PFLANZEN SIE IHRE EIGENE MEDIZI

INTRODUCTION

We will likely all remember the "Great Toilet Paper Crisis" of 2020. The Coronavirus Pandemic was declared, and the world went into lockdown. Critical supplies like toilet paper, canned goods, flour, and just about every other staple were snapped up by nervous people looking to provide for their families in a very uncertain time. I was very fortunate to have had my dear friend Margot warn me several weeks before the lockdown to stock my pantry, and I did. Even still, I bought some completely overpriced toilet paper on Amazon, just in case.

"Just in case" is a great motto for those who want to be self- sufficient. When we are caught unaware or unknowledge- able about how to provide essentials for our families, it adds stress to an already difficult situation.

Shortly after the grocery shelves were all cleared off, I began paying attention to our neighborhood Facebook group chat. I realized that local parents were looking for medicine for their sick children. Who had Children's Tylenol? Who had Children's Advil? Who knew of a drugstore that had some still in stock? If the pharmacy was out of stock, what were they to do? For me, this reinforced the need to be knowl- edgeable about the herbs, spices, and foods I grow in my garden. I needed to be a self-sufficient family guardian. Many scared parents didn't know other possible ways to deal with fever, toothache, or ear infections. Many of us have never been taught or even had the opportunity to learn these critical skills.

In my first book, *The Homestea•er Herbal Han•book,* I mentioned my journey to health. I grew up never knowing anything about growing food, and I never hesitated to pop a pill to treat a headache or fill a prescription for any malady. I didn't know there were green alternatives. But later in life, after continual bouts of illness and a weakened immune system, I started to look beyond the pharmaceutical industry to seek alternatives. Quite frankly, I just wanted to feel better. As I had the opportunity to grow my own food, herbs, and spices, I began to learn about their power to promote health and treat some basic medical and health needs, act as first aid alternatives, and even their ability to heal more serious conditions. I also began to watch people struggle with the side effects of their prescriptions and was convinced there had to be something better than relying exclusively on pharmaceuticals.

A classic example is what happened to one beautiful lady in my neighborhood. My young neighbor shared with me her struggle with depression and how the antidepressants she was taking did not make her feel better—how the side effects were crushing her.

Have you ever looked at the potential long-term side effects of antidepressants? You risk feeling emotionally numb, gaining weight, reducing your positive feelings, and experi- encing sexual problems. When you look at it this way, even antidepressants can be depressing!

> *"Big Pharma nee•s sick people to prosper. Patients, not healthy people, are their customers. If everyone was cure• of a particular illness or •isease, pharmaceutical companies woul• lose 100% of their profits on the pro•ucts they sell for that ailment..."*
>
> *— JAMES MORCAN*

All businesses need to make a profit, but it is a sad world when any company thrives off the sick. What does it mean when we have to take one medication to ease the effects of the first? We are stuck between a rock and a hard place. It's impossible to ignore our health problems, so we lay our trust in the conventional medicines these companies mass produce. If there are side effects, we must put up with them for the sake of our well-being.

Ironically, many people don't even experience the side effects of medication because they cannot afford to pay for their prescribed drugs. The term "Medication Insecurity" was coined because many people struggle with the cost of their prescriptions. Between January 2018 and January 2019, 22.9% of American adults said they or someone in their household couldn't pay for their prescribed medications. It breaks my heart to read that over 13% of Americans know someone who has died in the last five years because they couldn't afford medical treatment (Fortunato, 2020).

Whether you can't afford to pay for medication or aren't happy with pumping yet more chemicals into your body, you can't ignore the problem. At some point, you or your family members will get sick. It might be something ordinary like a cold or allergies, and it might be short-term, like muscle aches and pains, or it could be chronic. If the pharmacy is your first and last resort, you will be thrilled to hear of an alternative solution.

You might think there is some new alternative that nobody has heard about, but the truth is, the answer lies in nature and centuries of tradition all over the world—herbs! Since the dawn of time, man has been using herbs to heal a wide range of ailments, and thanks to these herbs, we have many of our conventional medicines today.

You will learn how to take care of your family with the help of your backyard or even just your window-box garden. We will examine what herbs and spices can prevent and even cure certain illnesses. We will also understand more about plants that won't cure a chronic disease but will help you to manage symptoms for a better quality of life.

Years ago, as a rookie gardener, my friend Margot joked that the only thing that grew in my garden was the death rate! I made every mistake under the sun. I didn't know what I didn't know! I wasn't taught how to do this. (Or perhaps I should say I didn't pay attention to what I was taught.) I needed help and knowledge and someone to teach me how. If you can relate to this, you will be pleased to follow 5 very simple, proven steps to grow your plants and various tech- niques to create your remedies, whether for you, your chil- dren, or your friends and family. Start your self-sufficient journey here.

You don't have to keep living with the aches and pains that prevent you from enjoying your hobbies. Stress and anxiety shouldn't be the new norm, and left unresolved, they will impact all other areas of your life. Furthermore, many diseases we associate with old age can be minimized or prevented. Isn't it best to start now, promote overall health, and prevent as many illnesses and diseases as possible?

Before you begin to worry that I am some flower child who resists all things modern, I am far from it. I was one of the biggest skeptics, but by trusting science and tradition, I was able to change my life. I will share the same science and tradition that I learned so that you can use herbs in the safest way possible. I am also very aware that each of us is unique, and there is no "one-herb" solution for all. Whenever I find a new study or herb I want to try, I always consult my doctor, and if you take any medication, I urge you to do the same.

Sometimes, it is irresponsible to stop taking your prescribed medication and start an herbal one. That doesn't mean herbs won't help. It means that the power of herbs needs to be respected. There will be more on this in subsequent chapters.

It took me years to appreciate the benefits of my garden. I made the rookie mistake of getting too excited and planting too many things at once, and I have burned more syrups than you can imagine. But all these experiences keep teaching me more and more about the incredible power of nature. Writing a book was never on my list of goals but helping others always has been.

After the kind feedback from my first book, my passion blossomed (bad pun, I know). Sharing this new information with you isn't only fun – it's exciting because I know how much your life & health can change too.

So, as keen as you are to start growing herbs and trying out each incredible remedy, it's essential to know how herbs work and why pharmaceuticals seem to get so much of the limelight.

SECTION ONE:

THE BASICS

"The flavors an• fragrances of herbs play an important role in the healing process, as •oes the respect an• care the gar•ener uses when ten•ing, collecting an• preparing the herbs into me•icine"

— DEB SOULE

1

PHARMACEUTICALS VS. HERBALISM

We place a lot of faith in conventional medicine. Don't get me wrong; I have nothing against doctors, and I am grateful for their knowledge and expertise and have relied on it many times. However, it is good to question what alternatives exist. Every time we fill a script and "pop a pill" because someone advises us to, pharmaceu- tical companies make a profit. But do we ever question what is in these little pills? Well, finally, we are starting to ask those questions.

More and more people are looking for herbal solutions. So much so that Americans spend $1.5 billion each year on dietary supplements and vitamins (Spraul, 2020). It's become increasingly challenging to take all the necessary vitamins and minerals from our diets alone. And while supplements are a good start, we must still trust a company and believe the claims their herbs have been grown and prepared in the best environment (at a price, of course) before we use their herbs. On the other hand, a packet of seeds costs a gardener around $3 and can last a lifetime. But let's not get ahead of ourselves.

WHAT EXACTLY IS HERBAL MEDICINE?

Herbal medicine, also known as botanical medicine or phytotherapy, uses plant parts such as leaves, berries, roots, bark, and flowers to create drugs &

treatments. Today, there are around 350,000 plant species, and more than 53,000 have active ingredients that can improve our health (Pan, et.al., 2014).

The first evidence of herbal medicine dates back to 60,000 years ago. Yarrow and chamomile were found on Nean- derthal tooth plaque. Years after this, Veda Vyasa and others compiled the Vedas. This is a collection of hymns and poems written around 3500 BC. The Atharva Veda deals with ancient remedies, many of which are still used today. *Ayurve•a* is Sanskrit for "the science of life" and contains more than 300 herbal remedies.

Approximately 1000 years later, the Chinese began to make significant contributions, although Traditional Chinese Medicine wasn't documented until around 250 AD.

It was Hippocrates who made an impact on medicine in the West. Before the Father of Medicine wrote his herbal findings, people used to believe that sickness and illnesses were a curse from God. Hippocrates was so unpopular for putting forward his alternative suggestion that he spent 20 years in prison, where he wrote *The Complicate• Bo•y*. One of the plants he wrote about was the willow. A few centuries later, we used willow bark to make aspirin.

Herbal medicine grew in popularity, especially from the 15th to the 18th century, when Latin and Greek books were translated into English. But the late 19th century and early 20th century saw things turn for the worse. Herbalism became associated with witchcraft, as demonstrated through the Salem Witch Trials. From 1910 to 1935, medical schools weren't allowed to teach homeopathy, or they would lose their accreditation. At the same time, science was uncov- ering more about extracting active ingredients to make conventional medicine, so the need for herbs fell.

HOW DO HERBS BOOST HEALTH?

Plants have a range of phytochemicals that help them stay healthy and resist fungi, bacteria, and viral infections. There are two classes of phytochemicals that interest researchers— carotenoids and polyphenols. Flavonoids are a type of polyphenol and have become increasingly important in our diet because they are high in antioxidants. Our busy, stressful lifestyles today, coupled with exposure to numerous chemicals and toxins, make the body more prone to create free radicals that cause oxidative stress. Due to lifestyle and environmental influences, it's easy for the body to have a greater risk of having more free radicals than antioxidants. This is when we are at the most significant risk for chronic disease.

By increasing our intake of herbs and spices, we can consume more of these active ingredients and boost our health without paying for conventional medicine. What is important is learning which plants contain the most benefi- cial active ingredients you or your family require.

PHARMACEUTICALS STEALING THE SHOW

Let's look at two popular examples that are both steeped in history. The poppy, now most commonly recognized as a symbol of remembrance of World War I, has been used as a painkiller since around 2100 BC. Traditionally, the milky liquid in unripe seed pods was scraped out and air-dried to make opium. Opium contains 9-14% morphine (PubChem, n.d.). Opium is also used to make heroin and codeine; both are used for pain relief. It's not really fair that Friedrich Wilhelm Adam Sertürner gets all the credit for morphine. Credit where credit is due, and while it is incredible what scientists have achieved with the advancement of plant- based drugs, they wouldn't have gotten so far without plants or the experience of previous generations who used poppy to ease their pain.

Foxgloves are beautiful flowers, and centuries ago, the leaves were dried and ground into a powder to cleanse the internal body and as part of an ointment to treat wounds. Today, digitalis is the compound extracted from dried foxglove leaves and used to make heart medications such as Digitoxin and Digoxin. These medications are cardiotonic and can strengthen the heart muscle and improve circulation in those who suffer from congestive heart failure.

I find it perplexing in just one century, thousands of years of proven herbal remedies were replaced with modern scien- tific discoveries.

These discoveries significantly improved our health in certain areas but overwhelmed us with side effects and other health issues on the other. And these are only two examples. Scientists, specifically giant pharmaceu- tical companies, credit themselves for something found in the wonderful world of nature. Nevertheless, we don't want to mess with mother nature!

SPECIAL CONSIDERATIONS WHEN USING HERBAL REMEDIES

Herbs contain powerful active ingredients that greatly benefit our overall health. But we must use caution and common sense when using them. There is a reason the FDA hasn't approved the use of all herbal medicines indiscrimi- nately. A few plants, like foxglove, contain phytotoxins, which cause some nasty, potentially lethal effects. This is why we can't just go around picking any pretty flowers and making herbal teas. Scientists can carefully extract the desired compound from a flower or herb and discard the harmful component. However, we laypeople need to exercise caution!

On the one hand, this is good because we know the product is safe. On the other hand, an herb can have numerous other benefits we don't get when we rely on conventional medi- cine. It's unlikely that your heart medication contains the same vitamins, minerals, and antioxidants as herbs, but we must exercise great caution before playing with such life- critical pills!

When we use an herbal remedy, we use all the active ingredi- ents. It is challenging for scientists to understand how this combination of ingredients will interact with different human bodies. It's even harder to know how these compounds will react to the various medications on the market today. Therefore, always ask a doctor before using herbal medicine if you take any medication.

The same can be said for anyone who has liver or kidney disease because your body may not break down all types of medication the same way. If you are scheduled to have surgery, you should also check with your doctor in case the herbs you use potentially interact with anesthesia or other medications used during the procedure. Some can also impact the body's ability to clot blood.

The use of herbal medicine with children, pregnant women, and women who are breastfeeding should also be overseen by a doctor or at least used with great caution. More and more studies prove the benefits of herbs with adults, but as you can imagine, there aren't as many pregnant women or parents willing to offer themselves or their children up as guinea pigs. Again, that's not to say that there aren't many safe herbs and spices that we can easily use.

Another thing to consider is that growing your own organic herbs and spices and preparing your own remedies isn't the same as buying supplements. The FDA doesn't regulate supplements. As such, big box stores can get away with selling falsely advertised products. For example, studies have shown there is no echinacea found in certain Walmart echi- nacea supplements and no St. John's wort found in some Target St. John's wort supplements—even with those names on the label (Bionic Products, 2016). However, when you grow your own plants, you know precisely what is going into your and your family's bodies. I recently attended a seminar that recommended growing all your plants from seed because even plants grown in a nursery may not be produced in the most healthy conditions. The instructor even mentioned a well-known chemical fertilizer that contains copper sulfate, a known carcinogen. If the goal is health, how much better is it to control what plants you grow and what natural products you use to promote that growth?

One thing to keep in mind, there is no guarantee that one herb will have the same effect on you as it does on the next person. Imagine two people who start taking St. John's wort for mild depression. After a couple of weeks, one notices a difference, and after a month, the second person doesn't. It doesn't mean that this herbal remedy doesn't work. It simply means that one person didn't find the right one for their body. Fortunately, we will discuss so many herbs you will have plenty to choose from.

Also, don't feel that you will be drinking five different herbal teas daily for the rest of your life. We can do many things with the plants we grow, and we will look at these next.

2

GETTING CREATIVE WITH HERBAL REMEDIES

***REMINDER:** Before you rea• this chapter, have you •ownloa•e• your **full-color** reference gui•e to all the herbs we •iscuss in this book? When you rea• about an herb, it is helpful to see it an• know what we are talking about.*

Scan this bar co•e

Or go to

referenceguide.homesteadmindset.com

to get your copy. An• if you have any •ifficulties, email me •irectly at hello@ homestea•min•set.com

You will need some basic equipment to make more than herbal teas. One of the main benefits of building up your own pharmacy is saving money, so please don't feel you need to go out and buy expensive equipment. Syrups and salves were around way before the candy thermometer was invented, and although they might be handy, I have survived without one.

What I would advise is to start saving all the jars and tins possible. Also, if you have any children's medicine with droppers to administer drops, these will be ideal for one particular remedy we will learn how to make. Let's start with the simplest way to boost your health, which will also serve as a base for later creations. To avoid sounding repetitive, always use sterile jars to store your remedies.

THE DIFFERENCE BETWEEN AN HERBAL TEA AND A DECOCTION

Teas, infusions, and decoctions use hot water to extract water-soluble phytochemicals. Hot water is necessary because it breaks open the glands and cells in a plant allowing more benefits to seep into the water. The main difference is the time the plant parts steep in water.

The general ratio is 1 tablespoon of plant parts for 1 cup of water. Once you have tried a couple of times, you can increase the amount if you want to but start small in case of allergic reactions. Always strain the herbs after.

Herbal tea is the same as a regular cup of tea. Flowers, leaves, berries, roots, or bark are in hot water for 5 to 7 minutes. Naturally, the longer the plant parts are left to steep, the more benefits you will get and the stronger the tea will taste.

An infusion requires a longer steeping time, even until the water completely cools. Berries and seeds should be left for a minimum of 30 minutes, flowers for a couple of hours, and bark and roots for up to 8 hours.

Decoctions are more potent versions of infusions. Add your herbs and cold water to a saucepan. Bring the water to a boil and let it simmer for 25 to 45 minutes. Softer parts of the plants need less time, but roots and bark will need the full 45 minutes.

INFUSING OILS FOR CULINARY AND TOPICAL USE

When working with oils for either cooking or healing, you can choose from different types of oil, but I prefer olive oil because you can use the same infusion as a top-quality cooking oil and for topical use. You may also want to try almond oil, coconut oil, or canola oil. There are two methods for infusing oils, and the choice doesn't depend on the type of herb, spice, or oil. The simplest method is called solar infusion. Take a jar, add the herbs or spices you want to use, and fill it until about 3 inches of space is left. Pour in the oil of your choice so that all the herbs are well covered. If herbs stick out of the oil, try to poke them in or add more oil. Parts that are not in the oil could start to form mold. Seal the lid and place the jar in a brown paper bag on a windowsill. The jar will benefit from the warmth, and the brown paper bag will protect it from direct sunlight. It will take 2 to 3 weeks to infuse the oil, and it will help if you shake the jar regularly.

You can also create a double burner with a heat-proof container (glass is better than metal) in a saucepan of boiling water for a faster infusion. Add the herbs and oil to the container and let the water simmer for 1 to 5 hours. With both methods, strain the herbs from the oil before using it.

USING ALCOHOL FOR A TINCTURE

Tinctures can provide some of the most potent benefits because alcohol will extract compounds that aren't water- soluble. The alcohol you choose will, to an extent, depend on your preferences or even what you already have at home. Vodka is a popular choice because the flavor is neutral, but you can use whichever hard alcohol you prefer. What is more important, though, is the strength of the alcohol. The minimum strength to use is 20% ABV (alcohol by volume) or 40 proof. The ideal strength is 40 to 60% ABV or 80 to 120 proof. Typically, you take a few drops of tincture a day, so there is not enough alcohol to have an intoxicating effect.

Again, you have two methods to make a tincture. The first is the same as an infused oil: put your herbs in a jar and fill it with alcohol. If you prefer a more calculated approach, the second method uses one part of herbs to five parts of alco- hol. For both methods, ensure the herbs are completely covered and keep the jar in a cool, dark place for 4 to 6 weeks. Shaking the jar on a regular basis will help. Strain before storing and use.

TONIC WINES

Tonic wines are an interesting way to add health benefits and additional flavor to standard wine. One of the most famous tonic wines is the British mulled wine—a mixture of red wine, cloves, cinnamon, and oranges drunk warm during the winter.

You can make tonic wines the same way you would a tinc- ture. Most people prefer to use a sweeter wine, red or white. Some good herbs for tonic wines are lemon balm, ginger, peppermint, cinnamon, and borage.

SYRUPS FOR THE FAMILY

If you have any leftover decoction, you are halfway to creating a syrup. The good thing with syrup is that the added sweetener makes these herbal remedies last much longer. A decoction will last 48 hours in the fridge, but a syrup lasts up to 2 or 3 weeks.

To make a syrup, start with the herbs you wish to use and make a decoction. Remember, the longer you leave the herbs simmering, the stronger it will be, and so will the syrup. When your decoction is ready, strain the herbs. Next, you need to add a sweetener—typically honey or sugar. Honey is healthier, but neither will impact the effectiveness of your syrup. The ratio is 1:2, so 1 cup of sweetener to 2 cups of decoction. You can see now that this is a lot of sugar, which is not a good solution for people with diabetes. Once the decoction starts to reduce and thicken, you can transfer it into a sterile jar. Some people will add some tincture to the syrup, but then it's not suitable for children.

Most people take 1 to 3 teaspoons daily, depending on their symptoms. Don't forget there are plenty of things you can do with your syrup. You can add it to pancakes, ice cream, or yogurts. You can substitute it in your tea instead of honey or sugar, and syrups make an excellent addition to carbonated drinks.

SALVES FOR SKIN CONDITIONS

Once you have infused oil, there are only a couple more steps to making a homemade salve. It's important to ensure your infused oil has all the herbs your skin needs, but don't worry about waste. You will learn to grow an abundance of herbs, so don't worry about using too much.

Add 1 cup of infused oil in a double boiler and gently warm it. Pour in ¼ cup of beeswax. I like to use wax pellets because they are super handy to store and easy to use. Once the beeswax has melted, dip a spoon into the mixture and pop it into the freezer for a couple of minutes until it cools. This allows you to test the consistency before pouring it into a pot. Add more beeswax or oil, depending on your prefer- ences. More beeswax will make it thicker, whereas the oil will make it thinner.

The salve will cool and harden quite quickly, so it's best to transfer it as soon as the test is done. Don't let any water mix in with your salve because it could cause mold and shorten the shelf life, typically around six months or longer if kept in the fridge.

POULTICES AND COMPRESSES

Both a poultice and compress are applied directly to the affected area. This can be muscle and joint pains, wounds, bruises, or even on the forehead for headaches and migraines. Which method you choose will often depend on what supplies you have on hand because the main difference is how they are made.

For a compress, begin with a decoction. Dip an entire cloth into the decoction and place it on the body part you want to treat. It's good to leave it for at least 30 minutes and use the same decoction throughout the day, two or three times if need be.

A poultice uses herbs mashed up, typically in a pestle and mortar. If you don't have one, a super simple trick is to use the end of a rolling pin and a bowl. Add small amounts of water until the herbs become a paste. Cover the affected area with the paste, then wrap it in a bandage or plastic wrap. The ideal time to leave the poultice is 10 to 15 minutes and repeat it later in the day if necessary.

TAKING CARE WITH ESSENTIAL OILS

Essential oils are the most potent form of plant extract, so care should be taken. Many are so strong that they can't be ingested and are only used topically, inhaled, or in diffusers and baths. They are obviously beneficial, but with so many options, essential oils tend to be my last solution for herbal remedies. Plus, they take a lot of work for a small amount, and you will need a slow cooker.

Half-fill your slow cooker with the herbs of your choice and top this up with distilled water until it is ¾ full. Put the lid on but upside down; the concave shape encourages the steam that forms on the cover to condense and drip back into the pot. It will take 3 to 4 hours on low heat before you turn it off and let it cool. If you can fit the slow cooker in the fridge, great; if not, pour it into a bowl. Leave it in the refrigerator overnight.

The following day, you will notice a film of oil on top of the water. You need to gently separate this oil and store it in a container.

If you can't wait for your herbs to grow, you can start making herbal remedies with what you already have in your home. It is a great way to start using up store-bought herbs and spices so that you can replace them with your home- grown ones. Don't forget to label everything with the herb type and the date you made it.

Now that you know exactly how to make some incredible homemade natural remedies, it's time to look at the exten- sive list of herbs, starting with what you should grow to make a complete first aid kit.

SECTION TWO

YOUR VERY OWN FIRST AID KIT

"All the degrees, certificates, and training will only take you so far. To be able to heal, you need a well-stocked first-aid kit."

— UNKNOWN

When you move into your first home, you quickly learn that there are certain things you should always have on hand: a decent screwdriver, spare light bulbs, extra batteries, etc. The first aid kit falls onto this list of grown-up necessities—even more so when you have children. Cuts, burns, headaches, coughs, and colds can easily be treated, and the last thing you need is a trip to the pharmacy. In this section, we will cover the essentials to make sure you are prepared for those minor medical emergencies.

3

HERBAL TREATMENTS FOR WOUNDS

My grandchildren can be a little dramatic when it comes to cuts and scrapes. (Some more than others, but I won't name names!) Treating the wounds gives them time to calm down and gives me peace of mind that the wounds are clean and protected from infections. My favorite herbs are those with antibacterial properties and those that can speed up the healing process. Let's discuss a few good ones to keep on hand.

ALOE VERA – ALOE BARBADENSIS

Aloe vera is used in dozens, if not more, of over-the-counter products primarily to help with sunburn and as a key ingre- dient in cosmetics. The funny thing is, if you open an Aloevera leaf, you will notice that the gel isn't green! So, who knows why commercially sold products are?

The plant contains glycoproteins and polysaccharides. Glycoproteins help reduce inflammation and pain, while polysaccharides encourage skin repair and growth. A study involving 371 patients showed that Aloe vera could reduce wound healing time by 8.79 days (Maenthaisong, et. al., 2006).

The gel has strong antibacterial, antifungal, and antiviral properties, making it excellent for burns and cuts. Aloe vera can be placed directly on the skin. It also makes an excellent salve and poultice.

CALENDULA – CALENDULA ARVENSIS

Calen•ula officinalis is part of the daisy family and is some- times called a pot marigold. You can eat the flowers and leaves, but the leaves are a little bitter, so it is best to add them sparingly to leafy green salads. The most benefits are in the flower petals; for wounds, it's good to use them to infuse the oil.

For healing wounds, calendula is rich in antifungal and antimicrobial properties that can reduce the chances of infections and help with the healing process. Although it is effective alone, studies have shown that the results are considerably better when you combine calendula oil with Aloe vera (Eghdampour, et. al., 2013). It can help relieve irritated skin and encourage skin healing after bites and stings. Poultices, compresses, and salves are great ways to use calendula.

MARSHMALLOW – ALTHAEA OFFICINALIS

Herbal medicine typically uses the root of this plant, but the leaves have also been used to apply directly to wounds or in a poultice. The root produces a sap-like substance and is what was used to make the sweet treat of the same name. It is also high in antioxidants. This substance has numerous benefits for the body, particularly for the skin. The sap creates a protective coating that can reduce topical irritation. It may also help with sunburn and damage caused by UV rays but should not be used as a substitute for sunscreen.

Studies on humans are limited, but there have been positive results with rats. The extract was used to treat cuts, and compared with control groups, the healing was much improved (Rezaei, 2015). The root can also reduce the healing time because of its anti-inflammatory and antibacte- rial properties.

To make marshmallow infusions, you should use cold water. Unlike most herbs, the active ingredients in marshmallow root are better extracted with cold water. Dry the root and then chop lightly before soaking it in water.

ECHINACEA - ECHINACEA PURPUREA

We will look at other uses of echinacea (for the immune system, etc.) because this North American flower is another all-around star. Also known as purple coneflower, all parts of this plant can be used.

Echinacea is good for wound healing because of the chemi- cals alkamides and chicoric acid and their anti-inflammatory and antimicrobial properties. The body's first response to a wound is to trigger an inflammatory response. Those under a lot of stress may find their immune system slower to react, so healing is delayed. Echinacea is great for boosting the immune system.

In one study, the use of an echinacea tincture was used to test the healing of wounds in mice. One group of mice was "stressed," and the other was "non-stressed." The stressed group healed faster with the echinacea extract than the other group (Zhai, et. al., 2009). Common medicinal uses include poultices, compresses, and salves for wounds.

GOTU KOLA - CENTELLA ASIATICA

Gotu kola may be unfamiliar to some, but it is one of the popular herbs in Traditional Chinese Medicine and Ayurvedic medicine. It is typically used in Asian cuisine and is a member of the parsley family.

For the skin, there are antimicrobial and anti-inflammatory compounds, as well as triterpene. Triterpene is thought to stimulate collagen and new blood vessel production around wounds. You may also find that this leafy herb can help with stretch marks and scars. Gotu kola is most effective as an extract, so you can make oils, tinctures, or extract the essen- tial oils for the skin.

PEPPERMINT – MENTHA PIPERITA

All members of the mint family have antibacterial properties, but peppermint is considered the best. Peppermint has substantial amounts of l-menthol, menthone, menthyl, acetate, and limonene. I recently learned that the level of these active ingredients varies from region to region. For example, peppermint contained 12.7% menthone in Serbia, but in Turkey, it was 44.1%. In Korea, peppermint has as much as 64.5 to 94.2% limonene (Mancuso, 2020). The good news is that regardless of the compositions, they can all help with cuts and wounds.

Because peppermint has so many benefits, I tend to make a decoction for healing the skin and ensure I drink the leftovers.

COMFREY – SYMPHYTUM OFFICINALE

Comfrey is impressive because of the allantoins, rosmarinic acid, and tannins that help the skin to regrow and the anti-inflammatories that help with bruises and wounds. But this herb also comes with its warnings. Aside from its beneficial chemicals, comfrey also contains pyrrolizidine, which is highly toxic and may cause liver damage. Never take comfrey orally.

When using comfrey, only use low doses. Don't use too much, and don't simmer the water for too long. You also shouldn't use it on open wounds or areas where the skin is broken. If you are taking medication for the liver, don't use it, even on the skin, as the toxins can be absorbed through the skin. Children and pregnant women shouldn't use comfrey at all.

Comfrey made it on the list because it can be used to help with bruises, burns, sprains, and joint inflammation. A weak comfrey decoction can be dabbed onto bites and stings too. Because of the potential risks, you should only use comfrey for short-term applications.

The next part of our first aid kit will contain helpful solu- tions for those muscle injuries that can affect the whole family.

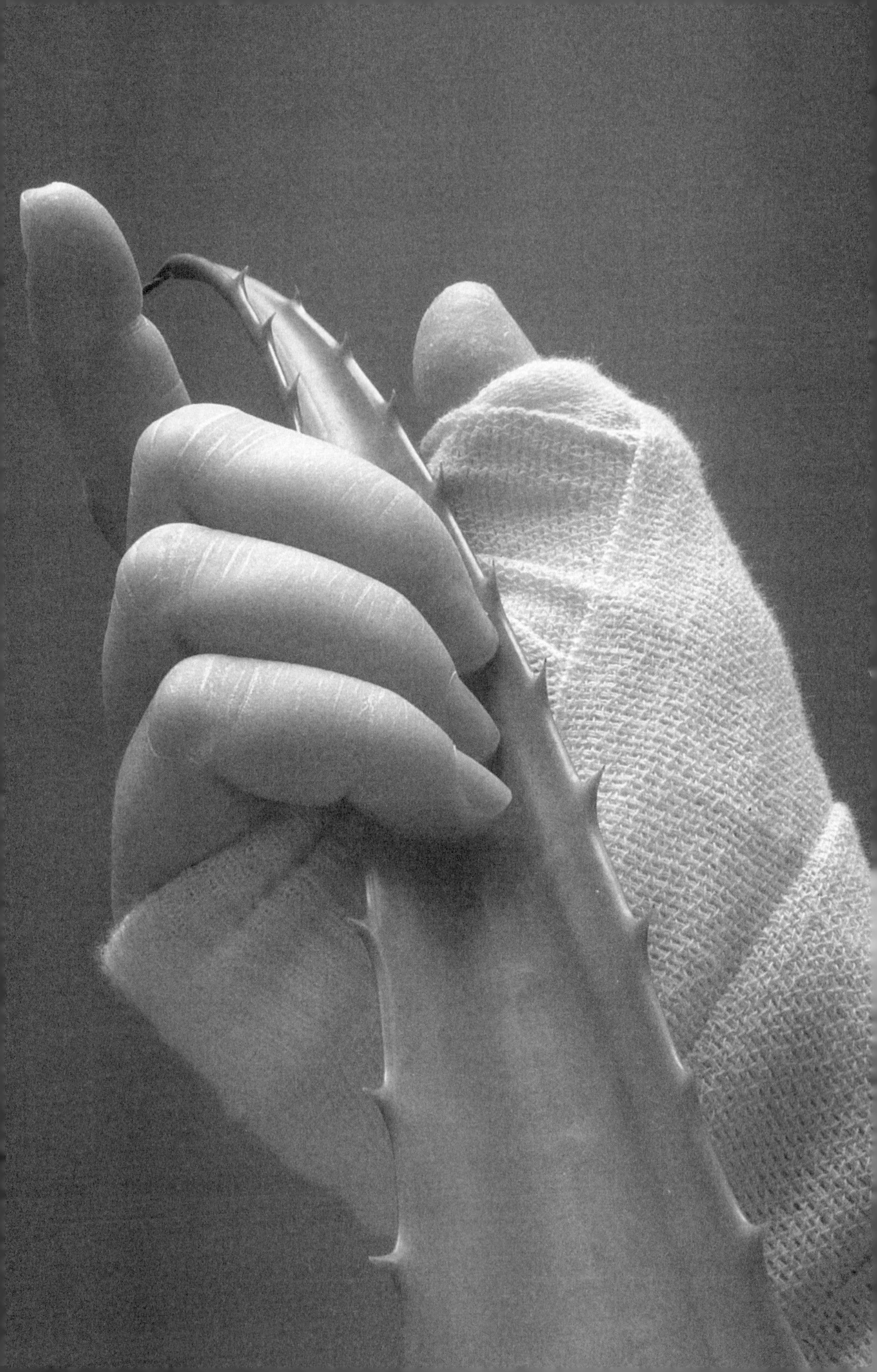

4

HOW TO TREAT THOSE ACHES AND SPRAINS

How many times have you heard the words "It's just a sprain?" Perhaps you've even said that yourself! It's supposed to be reassuring, but these injuries are painful. I remember watching my middle daughter Meghan roll her ankle playing senior basketball and then be carried off the court by her coach. She was on crutches for a couple of weeks and was devastated to miss her next couple of games. A sprain is a common injury, so whether it's older adults (like me) putting too much strain on their tendons or children coming home with sports injuries, you will want a remedy.

ROSEMARY - SALVIA ROSMARINUS

We take many herbs for granted, but rosemary is one that we should really explore because of its effectiveness. Aside from the delicious flavor, the anti-inflammatory properties can help muscles to relax and relieve pain.

Rosemary oil can help relieve sore muscles after a workout. A recent study used rosemary essential oils to alleviate muscle pain and swelling in women who weren't active. Pain and swelling were significantly reduced for up to 48 hours after the workout (Rezaee, et. al., 2019).

Rosemary oil or salve is a great part of your first aid kit to reduce different types of pain because of its ability. In addi- tion to using it on your muscles, you can also try it for headaches and joint pain caused by rheumatism or arthritis. Some people find the smell relaxing. A great benefit of having this member of the mint family on your skin is that it helps repel insects and reduces the chance of bites and stings.

To use rosemary as an essential oil, dilute it before rubbing it into muscles. You can also create an oil infusion for massages.

PEPPERMINT – MENTHA PIPERITA

We have already seen how peppermint has methanol, an active ingredient that creates a cooling effect on muscles and helps reduce pain. Again, it's not the only member of the mint family with methanol, but the higher levels are far more beneficial. Spearmint has around 0.05% methanol compared with 40% in peppermint.

The methanol in mint is responsible for many healing prop- erties and acts as an antispasmodic that can ease muscle spasms. Aside from using it topically, often in a salve, taking peppermint orally, like in a tea, can help with the muscle spasms caused by digestive problems such as irritable bowel syndrome.

EUCALYPTUS – EUCALYPTUS OBLIQUA

Most of us are familiar with using eucalyptus for colds and the flu, as inhaling it typically helps with congestion. As a native tree in Australia, Aboriginals used eucalyptus for fever, cuts, colds, and pain. It has antimicrobial, antibacterial, antifungal, antiviral, analgesic, anti-inflammatory, and anti-spasmodic properties. On top of that, it is also high in antioxidants. That's a lot of A's! This is all thanks to the main ingredient, 1,8-cineole, its aromatic component.

For pain, eucalyptus oil is good for muscle and joint pain. One study showed that inhaling eucalyptus oil after a total knee replacement reduced pain and blood pressure (Jun, et. al., 2013). You can also use the oil or salve for headaches and backache and possibly for lowering chronic pain. With all its benefits, eucalyptus is also handy to keep around for cuts and burns.

Euca is one of the essential oils that you cannot take orally. A few drops can cause nausea, vomiting, diarrhea, dizzi- ness, and/or drowsiness, and higher doses can cause a coma and even be fatal. That said, eucalyptus tea is safe to drink, but it's best to start with a weak brew to check for allergies.

GINGER – ZINGIBER OFFICINALE

I understand that not everyone is a fan of ginger, but it is worthy of the title "superfood." Fortunately, you now have several ways to use it rather than having to consume it. Although, I recommend experimenting with some recipes, especially with chicken! Ginger grows some absolutely amazing flowers, but it's the root of this plant that contains medicinal powers.

Many studies have focused on ginger supplements. For example, in one study, 74 adults with muscle pain caused by exercise were given either raw ginger, warmed ginger, or a placebo supplement for 11 days. The heat-treated ginger reduced pain by 23%, whereas the raw ginger reduced pain by 25% (Warner, 2010). The anti-inflammatory properties in ginger may be enough to help with nerve pain, and by improving circulation, you could even reduce the pain caused by leg cramps. As ginger also helps with nausea, pregnant women suffering from leg cramps will benefit by taking ginger daily.

If ginger isn't for your taste buds, you can try making ginger tea and adding other ingredients. Leave the rhizome (the root) in hot water for 10 to 15 minutes, and add lemon and a little honey. And if that is not appealing to you, chop up the rhizome, steep it in hot water to make a compress, or make a ginger paste for a poultice and use it three or four times a day. A poultice or compress can also help with backache and bruises.

FEVERFEW – TANACETUM PARTHENIUM

Feverfew takes a little extra knowledge to identify but is well worth the effort. It's easy to grow and isn't fussy about the soil type. Also, being a perennial, it just keeps coming back. Feverfew is a member of the daisy family but also goes by the names bachelor button, wild chamomile, and my favorite— flirtwort. You can tell the difference between a feverfew and a daisy because there are only around a dozen white petals on feverfew flower heads, and they are broader than a daisy's petals.

This little flower is special because it works in two ways. Apart from the anti-inflammatory properties, it might be able to reduce serotonin, which in turn slows down the production of histamine. Serotonin and histamine play a significant role in causing migraines. Out of 253 people that participated in a study taking 2 ½ feverfew leaves a day, 72% found that it helped prevent headaches. Additionally, nausea and vomiting caused by migraines also decreased or disap- peared. It took several months for this low dose to take effect, but participants found that their migraines soon returned when they stopped taking it (Bone, 2007).

This remarkable headache relief is all thanks to the parthenolide found in feverfew, a substance that helps with spasms in smooth muscle tissue. Because of this, you can also use feverfew topically to treat sore muscles, including arthri- tis. Salves and infused oils are best for massages.

If you are pregnant or breastfeeding, you shouldn't take feverfew because it could cause contractions. If you are on blood thinners, you shouldn't use it either. The daisy family tends to cause allergic reactions, so if you know you have reactions to plants like daisies, marigolds, and chrysanthe- mums, you may be allergic to feverfew too.

TURMERIC – CURCUMA LONGA

A relative of ginger, turmeric is another superfood that produces gigantic leaves and stunning flowers. Turmeric has gained much attention in recent years because of the powerful anti-inflammatory and antioxidant properties found in curcumin, the curcuminoid that gives this spice its color. It can help with muscle soreness and damage caused by exercise and can speed up recovery time.

We will discuss turmeric in more detail in other chapters. Still, you should be aware that the body finds it difficult to absorb curcumin, and there are relatively small amounts in turmeric. It's always important to add black pepper to your turmeric remedies. Black pepper contains piperine, and adding just 20mg of black pepper to 2g of turmeric can increase the absorption by up to 2,000% (Shoba, et. al., 1998).

Like peppermint, take as much advantage of this spice as possible. If you infuse the oil for massages, be sure to make extra for cooking.

Moving further up the body, let's take a look at some natural relief for when pain takes its hold on your head. It's hard to believe, but even the harshest of migraines can be helped with herbs.

5

NATURAL RELIEF FOR HEADACHES AND MIGRAINES

Headaches were one of those things for which I used to run straight to the medicine cabinet for some Advil. Rarely did I think about the type of headache; I just wanted it gone! Fortunately, mine have always been the tension kind and nothing I would consider severe. I feel bad for those who struggle with the pain caused by migraines, sinus headaches, or the incredibly intense pain brought on by cluster headaches.

There is an herbal solution for all, some of which we have already discussed, like rosemary, ginger, feverfew, and peppermint. We will take a quick look at a few others that act as natural painkillers.

LAVENDER – LAVANDULA SPICA

Lavender is a lovely plant for beginner gardeners because the less you fuss over it, the better it does. It requires a little more patience to grow it from seeds, so if you see a young plant, it's a good idea to buy one and transplant it into a container. For many people, the scent of lavender is a favorite for relaxing, with the added bonus of producing a scent that bugs can't stand!

Lavender oil, when inhaled, can reduce the pain caused by various types of headaches within as little as 15 minutes (Koulivand, et. al., 2013).

Simply rub two or three drops on the upper lip in the early stages of the headache. This is due to the active ingredients linalool, linalyl acetate, and like eucalyptus, 1,8 cineole. Linalool and linalyl acetate can also have a local anesthetic effect, so having a lavender salve at hand may also be helpful for burns, stings, and bites.

Don't forget; there is a difference between an oil and essen- tial oil. Studies used lavender oil. The essential oil is too strong to be used directly on the skin and needs to be diluted.

VALERIAN – VALERIANA OFFICINALIS

Valerian is a native perennial to Europe and Asia but toler- ates the cold well enough to grow in many zones. The plant produces different colored flowers in large clusters and can produce hundreds of seeds that will spread. In some parts of the world, it is classified as an invasive weed, so take care that it doesn't take over your garden.

Unlike the other herbs, valerian doesn't work as a painkiller. Instead, it helps to relieve some of the symptoms that can lead to migraines and tension headaches, including insom- nia, stress, anxiety, and depression. The volatile oil valerenic acid has a sedative effect and can help us cope with the stress of our daily lives. For this reason, you shouldn't use valerian if you take any other form of sleep medication or antide- pressants.

For herbal remedies, we use valerian root. When you are using the roots to make a decoction, don't simmer them. It's one of the few roots that do better with cold water extrac- tion because the heat can cause a loss in these important volatile oils.

CORIANDER – CORIANDRUM SATIVUM

Coriander and cilantro have very different flavors despite coming from the same plant. The cilantro leaves and stems have a citrusy taste that is best used fresh or added at the end of cooking to prevent that soapy flavor from coming through. The plant's seed—what we call coriander—is warmer and nuttier. The different parts of this herb have different health benefits too, so it's important to collect the seeds if you suffer from headaches.

The seeds are anti-inflammatory, anticonvulsant, hypo- glycemic, hypotensive, and analgesic. High levels of terpenoid linalool help the seeds to protect our brains. In Ayurvedic medicine, an infusion is made with the seeds, and the steam is inhaled, helping with sinus headaches. A syrup made from coriander seeds reduced the frequency and dura- tion of migraines as well as the levels of pain (Kasmaei, et. al., 2016).

HORSERADISH – ARMORACIA RUSTICANA

For years, the only thing I associated horseradish with was a delicious sauce to go with roast beef, but the roots of this vegetable do more than make a condiment. Horseradish has a powerful, spicy flavor but is not hot like chilies, more like an intense onion. It's actually a member of the mustard family, and it is really easy to grow in sun or partial shade and in pretty much any soil type. So, it is a good option for the newbie gardener.

It's because of the pungent smell and flavor, along with the high levels of sulfur, that help with sinus headaches. It boosts circulation in your face, clearing the upper respiratory passages. Aside from headaches, horseradish can help relieve the symptoms of a cold. If you can handle the flavor, put some freshly grated horseradish in your mouth, keep it there until the flavor disappears, and then swallow it. If this is too much, make an infusion or a decoction and drink a cup between meals.

HONEYSUCKLE – LONICERA CAPRIOFOLIUM

If you are a fan of helping hummingbirds and easing headaches, honeysuckle is a great choice. I am particularly nostalgic about honeysuckle, as my papa and nana grew it along their fence. As a child, I smelled it every time I went out to play in their backyard. The North American native trumpet honeysuckle is bright red with tubular flowers. However, there are many species. Honeysuckle can be either shrubby or climbing. If your variety is a climber, you will need to provide it with a support structure.

Honeysuckle can help with headaches and other types of pain because it contains salicylic acid, the same chemical taken to make aspirin. It also has the flavonoid luteolin—an antiviral, antioxidant, and anti-inflammatory.

Use the leaves, flowers, and berries for your homemade pharmacy, and the traditional use is to make a decoction. Be careful with large quantities of berries as they could cause mild poisoning. This also depends on the variety of honey- suckle, as some aren't toxic.

YARROW - ACHILLEA MILLEFOLIUM

Yarrow is a popular herb for herbalists today and for many practitioners throughout history. I am particularly fond of yarrow as the village I live in is named after this fantastic herb. It is used in Traditional Chinese Medicine and was popular in Europe thanks to the warrior Achilles, who is said to have treated his soldiers' wounds with yarrow. This is one of the reasons this herb is also known as a soldier's or mili- tary herb. These ingredients help stop the enzymes needed in the chemical reactions that lead to pain. At the same time, another ingredient called sesquiterpene lactones helps to lower the action of certain hormones that cause pain. This is a worthy herb because it can heal wounds and reduce many types of pain.

Eighty percent of the brain is water, so even the mildest dehydration can cause headaches. It is estimated that one in ten headaches is caused by a lack of fluids (Blau, et. al., 2004). It's a good idea to make teas and infusions from these herbs so that you are increasing your fluid intake and reducing the chance of dehydration at the same time.

6

SAY NO TO ANTIHISTAMINES

Winter has been long, and you are desperate to shed the layers and feel the sunshine on your face, only to remember that the next season is allergy season. Nobody gets more excited than we do when flowers start to bloom, but airborne pollen has the unhappy knack of making some people feel like they are permanently unwell, myself included. The itchy eyes, runny nose, and sneezing can also occur year-round when the airborne particles are things like dust or pet fur.

When these particles enter the body, the immune system kicks in to fight off the invading objects. This can cause inflammation. Two plants already on our first aid kit list can help with allergies. Ginger can help boost the immune system and act as a natural antihistamine, and the steam from ginger tea can help with congestion. Yarrow has antimicrobial and anti-catarrhal properties. Anti-catarrhal means it can help remove excess mucus. In this chapter, I will show you a few more interesting herbal remedies you can try.

STINGING NETTLE – URTICA DIOICA

Most people learn what a stinging nettle is the hard way, and this prickly little plant becomes an enemy. Few people know how healthy it is.

Stinging nettles have antioxidant, astrin- gent, antimicrobial, and analgesic properties. The leaves have an antihistamine effect by blocking the body's production of histamine and prostaglandin. As an anti-inflammatory, it can also help with the symptoms caused by allergies.

Nettles are packed with vitamins that can boost your all- around health. In particular, vitamins A and C can improve your immune system, vitamin B helps your energy levels, and vitamin K, as well as the mineral calcium, can help your bones.

We have such a nasty reaction to stinging nettles because they have tiny hairs filled with chemicals that irritate our skin. By boiling nettle leaves, you destroy these hairs, making them safe for consumption. The other benefit of boiling the leaves is that you already have a decoction to drink and inhale.

PERILLA – PERILLA FRUTESCENS

Although this is a less commonly known member of the mint family, you will find these green and purple leaves (also called purple mint) are an excellent addition to your garden. Like other mints, it's easy to grow and keeps pests away. The taste is slightly different from your traditional mint, with a bit of a nutty flavor. The leaves and seeds offer health bene- fits, but the flowers can be toxic in large doses.

Perilla is often used to treat asthma symptoms because it can improve lung function. Perilla oil is made from the seeds which contain alpha-linolenic acid. Several animal studies have shown the oil to reduce "allergic mediators," the chemi- cals that cause allergic reactions (Asif, 2011).

What comes as a more incredible surprise is that perilla oil has one of the highest levels of omega-3 of all plant oils. Omega-3 can help protect the body from various diseases, such as cardiovascular disease and Parkinson's disease. Combined with the antioxidants, perilla seed oil could suppress the growth of cancer cells, but more studies need to confirm this.

Inhaling the steam is the best way to take advantage of perilla. If you are weary of teas, add the leaves to your bath.

SEA BUCKTHORN - HIPPOPHAE RHAMNOIDES

Sea buckthorn was one of my favorite discoveries as a little gem for the herbal pharmacy. Before discovering why it's so fantastic (the power of the antioxidants), it's important not to confuse this shrub with buckthorn, a completely different plant. Sea buckthorn produces bright orange berries that will tickle your tastebuds with hints of sweet and sour. Use the seeds and berries for their health benefits. Though these benefits are different, you can create an infused oil with both parts of the plant. Buckthorn has small dark berries. The berries were once used to purge the body, but this is no longer the practice since the toxicity in the berries can make you feel very sick.

For allergies, sea buckthorn has superoxide dismutase, the most potent antioxidant, and it can improve respiratory, eye, mouth, and mucous membrane health. The seeds have a lot of anti-inflammatory properties and may improve your immune system. There is also a good amount of omega 7, which can be good for topical use on the skin. The berries have omega 3 and vitamins C and E too. Omega-3 will help as an anti-inflammatory, while all three can improve the immune system.

If you are interested in growing sea buckthorn, like most berry plants, the seeds need a period of cold stratification before sowing them in spring. To do this, place them in a zip lock bag with some moist soil and pop the sealed bag into the fridge for 90 days. This will speed up germination by mimicking what would typically occur during the winter months.

BUTTERBUR - PETASITES HYBRIDUS

You will need more space for this plant than your traditional culinary herbs, but it grows well in most zones, especially in moist areas. The butterbur leaves can be 1 to 2 feet in diame- ter, with the Japanese variety growing over 6 feet wide. Traditionally, these leaves were used to stop butter from melting. The plant produces an impressive cluster of flowers, but it is the leaves and stems that are used in herbal medicine.

Like our previous plants, butterbur works by preventing inflammatory chemicals such as histamine and leukotrienes that lead to an allergic reaction. One study showed that butterbur extract was as effective at treating allergic rhinitis (hay fever) as the medication cetirizine. The added benefit of butterbur was that it didn't cause drowsiness like cetirizine did with some people (Schapowal, 2002).

You can make a wide range of herbal remedies with butter- bur, from teas to tinctures. If you are suffering from migraines, you can use the plant's roots because they contain petasin, a compound believed to relax blood vessels in the brain.

Butterbur also contains pyrrolizidine alkaloids. These chem- icals may cause liver damage, so it's best to keep the use of butterbur short-term and not use it if you have liver disease. Also, if you are allergic to the ragweed family (daisies and marigolds), you should steer clear of butterbur.

Most people will find that the biggest discomfort from having allergies is the trouble with runny noses and conges- tion. For this, steam inhalation is perfect. But as all parts of the plant have additional nutrients, I would recommend using them to make tea, inhaling the steam, and then drinking the tea to take full advantage of these beneficial plants.

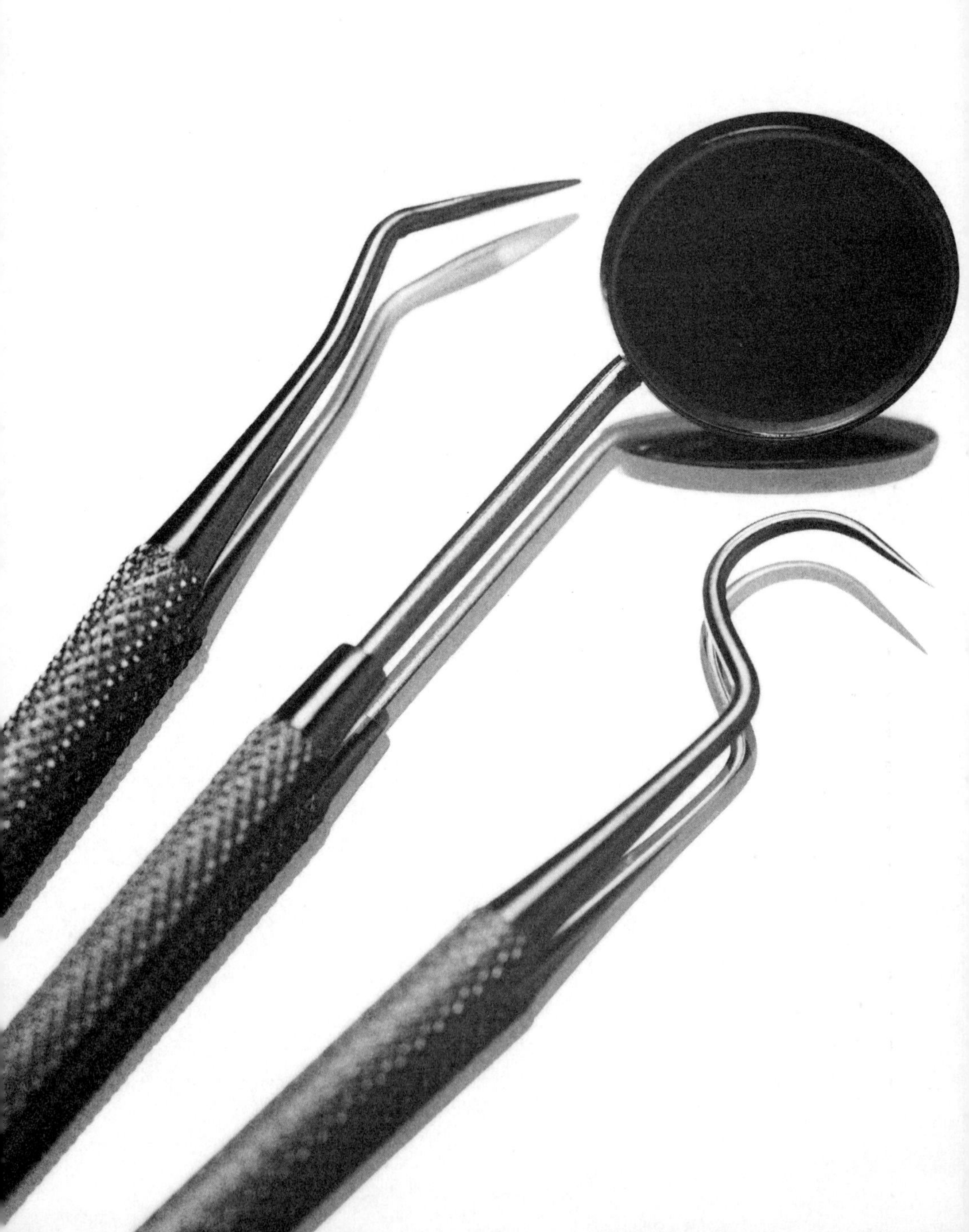

7

WHAT TO DO FOR THAT TOOTHACHE

I don't know anyone who can say they actually enjoy going to the dentist, but at the same time, almost anyone that has ever had a toothache would rather visit the dentist than suffer for much longer. We will finish this section with a brief chapter of some helpful remedies for when those teeth are causing you grief.

GINGER AND TURMERIC

Both these root spices have antibacterial and antiseptic properties and can help improve dental hygiene and reduce pain. The anti-inflammatory properties can relieve toothache caused by infections or swelling of the gums. At the same time, these spices can also reduce the bacteria in your mouth that can cause tooth decay. Less tooth decay means less risk of further toothache. This is especially true for ginger because the compound raffinose reduces the ability of bacteria to build up (Korea University, 2016).

There are a few ways you can use ginger and turmeric for toothache. For those who like the taste, you can cut a slice, place it on the sore tooth, and gently bite down, so the juice covers the tooth. With slices of ginger or turmeric, you can make a decoction, let it cool, and use the liquid as a mouth- wash. Or, if you have dried these spices and ground them into a powder, mix the powder into a paste with a little bit of water and rub the mixture around the aff

GARLIC – ALLIUM SATIVUM

When your toothache is severe, and you want an almost instant solution, you might have to put up with stinky breath! Garlic contains allicin, an impressive source of antibacterial and antiseptic properties, and it also has anti- inflammatories to help with pain relief.

The downside is that allicin is only created when garlic is crushed, sliced, or chopped. A whole clove of garlic doesn't have any allicin, nor does garlic powder. To use garlic for toothache, you can gently chew on a clove of garlic for around 10 minutes, as this is the time it takes for all the health benefits to be released. You can also chop it and add a little salt because it will also help kill bacteria. Rub the mixture on the painful tooth and gums.

Don't leave the garlic in your mouth for more than a couple of hours, as the potent compounds could end up causing a burning, tingling sensation in the mouth.

PEPPERMINT AND THYME

Unlike ginger and turmeric, which work well separately, peppermint and thyme are like the "power couple" for toothache, but if you only have one on hand, it can still help. The menthol in peppermint that helps with muscle aches has the same effect on toothaches, and all you need to do is chew on a couple of leaves. Thyme has antifungal and antiseptic properties that can help prevent gum disease and tooth decay.

To use the two together, you can make a paste by grinding fresh ingredients in a pestle and mortar with a bit of water or make a mouthwash with a decoction.

CHAMOMILE – MATRICARIA CHAMOMILLA (GERMAN) AND CHAMAEMELUM NOBILE (ROMAN)

There are two types of chamomile, and their healing proper- ties will sometimes vary. When it comes to toothache, both German and Roman chamomile can help. These plants contain chamazulene, so the extracts can be anti-inflamma- tory and antibacterial.

One study on German chamomile as a mouth rinse showed that 2 minutes of rinsing twice a day for four weeks reduced plaque and gingivitis without side effects or staining (Reza, et. al., 2005).

Apart from healing tooth infections, chamomile mouthwash can stop bleeding gums. Chamomile also contains a flavonoid called apigenin, a very handy sedative that can help you relax if you are nervous about the dentist. Chamomile is perfectly safe for children and may help them relax too.

A chamomile tincture is a great option for toothache because alcohol can help by numbing the area. For children, it's best to make a decoction, even adding a few drops of lemon juice for extra benefits. While warm, dip a cloth into the decoction and press it against the cheek. When the compress cools, dip it back in the warm decoction.

ALOE VERA – ALOE BARBADENSIS

I can imagine you cringing slightly at the thought of munching on an Aloe vera leaf. The taste is somewhat bitter, not to mention the spikes that need to be removed before eating the leaves! On the other hand, the gel has a very different, even refreshing, taste. While some people like to put it in smoothies for health benefits, you can rub the gel straight onto your teeth and gums.

Dentists have used aloe vera for a wide range of issues, such as canker sores, dry mouth, abscesses, and damaged gums. It's very effective at cleaning bacteria that get into cavities too. By blending Aloe vera gel with water, you can make a juice to gargle and help keep your teeth and gums healthy.

To use Aloe vera internally, you should wash the gel first. There is a yellow liquid called latex between the gel and the leaf, and latex can cause stomach upset. You would need to ingest quite a bit of this liquid to react, but it's better to be safe than sorry. Scrape the gel into a cheesecloth or coffee filter and gently run water over it.

Please remember that these are only going to be temporary solutions for toothache. You will likely need to see your dentist if you want to resolve the problem completely.

As we reach the end of our first section, you might feel a little panicked at the thought of growing over twenty herbs just for your first aid kit. And we haven't even started looking at other health conditions we need to address.

Please don't panic. When gardening, especially if you are a novice, don't stress yourself by planting too many things at once. The best thing about these herbs is their multiple benefits. So, for example, with just a couple, you can create a variety of remedies to keep in your first aid kit. You will have plenty of time to add more and more to your herb garden, and with a little experience, it will be far easier to get better growing results. In the third section, we will examine which herbs can help maintain good health and well-being and the importance of taking care of your immune system to prevent certain chronic diseases.

SECTION THREE

HERBS TO MAINTAIN AND BOOST HEALTH AND WELL-BEING

"You know, all that really matters is that people you love are happy an• healthy. Everything else is just sprinkles on the sun•ae."

– PAUL WALKER

In our fast-paced world, it's easy to forget the importance of health and happiness. Or perhaps it's not that we forget these things, but they get put to one side because so many other things take priority. And it's something we are guilty of doing at one point.

A healthy lifestyle can help prevent many serious conditions, such as diabetes, cancer, heart disease, mental health issues, and problems with joints and bones. Exercise and a balanced diet are key to a healthy lifestyle, but so are things like stress management. Even being healthy during pregnancy can reduce the risk of your baby having health problems.

This section will focus on self-care, like keeping your skin and hair radiant without spending a fortune on creams and masks. We also have a chapter on the best herbs to support your pregnancy and another chapter discussing how to take care of your immune system to prevent diseases associated with old age. Finally, we will look at ways you can treat yourself and enjoy some relaxing moments to recharge your batteries.

8

HOW TO KEEP THOSE SKIN FLARE-UPS UNDER CONTROL

In the previous section, we looked at how calendula, *Aloe vera,* and marshmallow help the skin heal from wounds and cuts because their active ingredients make them an excellent anti-inflammatory for skin irritations. All three can help reduce redness and itching, much like hydrocortisone cream, and they may also act as a moisturizer for dry skin. Moreover, all are generally great options for those with sensitive skin.

Lavender is another well-known treatment for skin irrita- tions and a popular cosmetic ingredient. Aside from headaches, lavender oil can do wonders for the skin. It can help with eczema and other dry skin conditions, fight acne and reduce its scarring, calm redness, and remove harmful toxins from the skin. Finally, lavender can reduce the effects of environmental stressors like UV rays and pollution, which might lead to wrinkles and dark spots. (Remember that lavender essential oil should be diluted before using it on the skin, but if you infuse the oil, you can add beeswax to create an effective skin salve.)

There are many reasons why your skin might be giving you grief, such as allergic reactions, rashes, stress, or an overac- tive immune system. Some skin conditions are also genetic. Dermatitis, the general term for skin irritations, comes from the words *derm* meaning "skin," and *itis* for "inflammation." The inflammation can cause unbearable itching that is enough to keep you up at night, which can harm other areas of your health. If you often rush to the pharmacy for a hydrocortisone cream, here are some natural solutions to consider.

CHAMOMILE – MATRICARIA CHAMOMILLA

Chamomile is a remarkable herb that can help your skin from the inside and outside. Its use for skin conditions goes back to Hippocrates's time when the ancient Greeks and Egyptians would use crushed flowers to heal weather-related skin irritations. Some centuries later, scientists have been able to pinpoint the differences in Roman and German chamomile and their effects on skin conditions.

Chamomile contains apigenin, an antioxidant that can help treat sunburn and rashes. It is particularly good at pene- trating deep into the skin to relieve inflammation that causes redness. Apigenin, bisabolol, and chamazulene make chamomile ideal for sensitive skin and eczema.

Regularly used antibacterial and astringent properties make this herb excellent for skin problems associated with various ages. For example, as an antibacterial, it can help to kill bacteria in the skin that may increase acne. As an astringent, chamomile tightens skin cells, making them smoother. Antioxidants can fight free radicals that lead to premature aging of the skin. Free radicals can cause oxidative stress, a possible cause of hyperpigmentation (dark spots on the skin). Regular use of chamomile can brighten these dark spots and give your skin a lovely glow.

Both types of chamomile contain the main components to help the skin, but German chamomile is preferred because it has higher levels of bisabolol and chamazulene. Studies have focused on German chamomile essential oil. A study on mice showed that four weeks of 100% pure organic German chamomile oil significantly reduced inflammation and itching (Lee, et. al., 2010).

There is no chamazulene in chamomile flowers. The only way to extract this ingredient is by distilling the flowers. Still, preparing chamomile in other ways will extract addi- tional skin benefits. Infusions, decoctions, and salves are best for targeted skin irritation, but drinking tea still gives you anti-inflammatory and antimicrobial benefits and is a way to heal your skin from the inside.

MILK THISTLE – SILYBUM MARIANUM

I confess that I have a strange obsession with this plant that many others almost detest. This plant can grow up to 6 feet tall, with a bright purple flower sitting on top of a green pod containing up to 6,000 seeds! Because it is so prolific and invasive, it's not everyone's favorite to grow. It can also be toxic to sheep and cattle, but for humans, the health benefits are extensive.

The power of milk thistle lies in the potent antioxidant and anti-inflammatory silymarin. It's so powerful against skin irritation that studies have shown milk thistle to reduce acute radiodermatitis (skin irritation that is a side effect of radiotherapy treatment) in breast cancer patients (Karbas- forooshan, et. al., 2018).

We will examine this herb for different chronic conditions, but for now, be sure to wear thick gloves when handling milk thistle. If you think this is a plant for you, be sure to deadhead flowers to reduce the risk of it taking over your garden.

NEEM – AZADIRACHTA INDICA

Neem, also known as Indian lilac, comes from a tree that can quickly grow to a large size in a short time—as much as 12 feet in just one year. There are dwarf varieties that can be grown in containers if you don't have that sort of space.

Containers can be moved indoors during the cold months, making them easy to grow in different climates.

The first records documenting the use of neem date back around 4,500 years ago, and the United Nations have named it the "tree of the 21st century." Over the years, various parts of the plant have been used to treat acne, psoriasis, eczema, ringworm, and warts (Kumar & Navaraham, 2013). Neem oil can also help with wrinkles, redness, and water loss in the skin. Rather than paying out for collagen skin creams to fight the signs of aging, you can make a neem oil that contains elastin, an enzyme that produces collagen.

The leaves are a good source of antioxidants, anti-inflamma- tories, and antibacterial properties. Still, the seeds and flowers are best for the skin because they contain palmitic, linoleic, and oleic fatty acids.

Neem leaves can be chewed to help clean the body of toxins and improve skin radiance. You can also use all parts of the plant directly on irritated skin or to make different types of infusions.

ST. JOHN' S WORT – HYPERICUM PERFORATUM

Most of the focus on St John's wort concerns depression and anxiety, but more recently, other mental health conditions like OCD, migraines, nerve pain, and different types of pain have also been explored.

There are tons of active ingredients in St John's wort, and we will look at some of these in section three, but for now, our main interest is the antioxidant hyperforin. This compound can help with mild skin irritations, rashes, cracked and dry skin, acne, and even eczema and psoriasis. St John's wort extract and petroleum jelly reduced inflammation in those suffering from mild to moderate psoriasis and atopic dermatitis (Mansouri, et. al., 2017).

The flowers contain the best medicinal properties. It's widely thought that the first St John's blossom is around the 24th of June, the birthday of St. John the Baptist.

With topical use, you must be careful if you have skin prone to sunburn. This herb can make the skin sensitive to sunlight, and you should either cover up or make sure you are using good sunscreen.

BURDOCK - ARCTIUM

Burdock and milk thistle are in the same family but have different genera. Like milk thistle, burdock is an impressive flower to grow with striking colors and prickly thistles. Unlike its purple partner, we use the roots of burdock for their health benefits.

The roots of burdock contain many active ingredients that benefit the skin. These include flavonoids, arcigen, and poly- acetylenes. On top of that, you have chlorogenic acid, an anti-inflammatory, and lactone, an antiseptic. These chemicals can reduce swelling, toxins, and acne. Finally, burdock root comes with inulin that brings moisture from deeper layers of the skin to the surface layer, helping relieve dry skin.

Burdock roots, once peeled, can be eaten raw or cooked. You can use them to make teas and tinctures or use them topi- cally as an oil.

The last thing you want to do is use an herbal remedy on your skin to make the condition worse because of an allergic reaction. Whenever you make a topical remedy, test it on a small patch of healthy skin. After a couple of hours, if there has been no reaction, you know you aren't allergic to the herbs you have chosen.

The next stage of self-care is giving your hair special atten- tion, whether to overcome an itchy scalp or add thickness and shine!

9

REVIVING HAIR AND ITS NATURAL SHINE

For some, the first thing people notice is a smile. For me, it's someone's hair. I marvel at everything from natural curls to shiny straight hair. My eldest granddaughter has the most beautiful thick, long hair that grows at a stun- ning pace, and my youngest has the most amazing tight curls and ringlets. I am fascinated by both! I used to constantly ask my friends what they did to get such luscious locks, but I soon realized I would rather spend an hour in my garden than at a hairdresser's, so it was time to grow some natural remedies.

Healthy hair doesn't just help you to feel more confident. It can tell you a lot about your health. Shiny, vibrant hair means your body is getting the essential nutrients it needs. On the other hand, dry or frizzy hair could mean that you are lacking in vital vitamins and minerals. Dandruff and hair loss aren't necessarily caused by stress, but stress can exacer- bate these conditions.

Herbs like lavender, *Aloe vera,* and chamomile will all benefit your hair. Here are six other herbs that make you feel like your hair is ready to star in that shampoo commercial.

GINKGO BILOBA

Ginkgo is the only surviving member of an ancient order of plants used in Traditional Chinese Medicine. It has green, fan-shaped leaves that turn bright yellow in fall. Though it is a tree, you can still grow it in containers and even as an indoor plant. Be warned, though, the female tree produces fruit that smells rancid, so it is best to move it outdoors during the fruiting season.

Gingko can help with various conditions related to the heart and blood flow, which can help dilate blood vessels so that blood flows more easily. This can help lower blood pressure and give the heart a break from having to pump so hard. The increased blood flow benefits the scalp, and more blood to the hair follicles encourages new growth, helping with hair loss caused by aging, postpartum hair loss, and alopecia.

There are lots of ways to use ginkgo. Some people like to grind parts into a powder and add them to cooking and smoothies. You can add some extract to your shampoo or create a decoction to use as a hair rinse.

ROSEMARY - SALVIA ROSMARINUS

Once you learn how versatile Rosemary is, you won't be able to resist growing it for more than cooking. Rosemary contains antioxidants and anti-inflammatories, with carnosic acid being the active ingredient for hair health. This chemical helps to heal tissue and nerve damage. Giving the nerves in the scalp a helping hand can lead to hair regrowth.

Comparing rosemary oil to the drug minoxidil, a commonly prescribed treatment for hair loss, both encouraged signifi- cant hair growth after six months. However, participants who used rosemary oil suffered less from an itchy scalp (Panahi, et. al., 2015). As a bonus, rosemary can also help moisturize the scalp and prevent premature graying. (Clearly, I should have started this earlier!) Still, please don't rush to cover your hair in rosemary essential oil, as you first need to dilute it in a shampoo or oil. You can make a decoc- tion to drink or use to rinse your hair, or you can make an infused oil.

DANDELION - TARAXACUM OFFICINALE

While not many people would think of growing dandelion on purpose because most people consider it a weed, these small plants contain a surprising number of nutrients. For the novice gardener, they are easy to grow, and for the impa- tient gardener, they can germinate in just ten days.

The roots of dandelion contain plenty of vitamins A, C, E, and B-complex. Furthermore, you can benefit from its choline, iron, magnesium, calcium, phosphorus, and potas- sium. All of these can promote strong, healthy hair.

Some types of hair loss, such as alopecia, are caused by inflammation. The body's immune system fights hair folli- cles as a defensive mechanism against what it thinks is a foreign invasion. One active ingredient in dandelion is poly- saccharides, an anti-inflammatory.

The best way to use dandelion roots is fresh or dry in a tea or decoction for drinking. This way, the body can absorb all the benefits this little plant offers. Though the roots have higher levels of nutrients, all parts are edible.

AMLA - PHYLLANTHUS EMBLICA

This one may come as a surprise, and although lesser known, it is considered a miracle worker for hair. Also known as Indian gooseberry, this tree can be grown in a pot. Remember that it likes warmer climates, so you might need to bring it indoors or use a greenhouse if you have one.

The fruit of an amla tree contains antifungal, antiviral, and antibacterial properties. These properties can help with scalp irritations and dandruff and improve scalp health. Calcium and vitamin C can stimulate hair growth, and vitamin C will boost antioxidants in the body. Healthy amla plants can contain 20 times more vitamin C than oranges (Times of India, 2021). Massaging amla oil into your scalp can strengthen the hair follicles and lower the risk of hair loss.

Amla berries have a unique flavor. They are both sweet and sour and crispy and juicy. You can try making a jam out of the berries or a delicious and nutritious juice. To make an oil, mash the fruit with a mortar and pestle. Strain it until you are left with just the juice. Add a carrier oil (coconut works well for your hair and face) and gently heat the oil and amla juice for 10 to 15 minutes.

HORSETAIL – EQUISETUM ARVENSE

One of the more appropriately named plants for healthy hair, horsetail, is a fern that looks like the mane and tail of a horse. It is a plant that can grow up to 20 inches tall, but the rhizomes spread like wildfire underground, so it's wise to grow it in a container.

Horsetail has an active ingredient not found in our other herbs, silica. Silica helps nails and hair to grow strong, and this plant has one of the highest amounts of this compound. Silica interacts with keratin, which can improve the struc- ture of your hair, even making it thicker. It is an antioxidant and enhances collagen production for overall hair health. Extracting the active ingredients can also encourage better blood circulation to help hair follicles get all these essential benefits.

You can use a few horsetail stems to make tea to drink, to add to your bath, or to use as a hair rinse.

STINGING NETTLE – URTICA DIOICA

I will quickly mention this plant for which I am gaining new respect. The antioxidants in stinging nettles may help boost circulation to the scalp for hair growth, and the nutrients can improve hair health. Nettles contain sulfur and silica, so a nettle tea or hair rinse can give your hair a natural shine without products. Don't forget to boil nettle leaves before doing anything with them, so they don't sting you.

Don't hesitate to use all these herbs to make a hair mask. You will have plenty of ingredients at home, including lemon juice, yogurt, banana, oils, honey, and egg whites. Mix it into a paste. Massage it into your scalp, then down to the ends of your hair. Force yourself to relax for 15 to 30 minutes while your homemade natural hair mask gets to work!

If you have been pregnant, you may have noticed some bizarre and beautiful changes to your hair. Some women get lovely thick hair during pregnancy and suddenly lose it after giving birth; others see an incredible shine once the baby is born. Aside from these herbs to help your hair, the next chapter will provide you with some ideas to help alleviate the typical problems many women experience in these joyful yet long nine months!

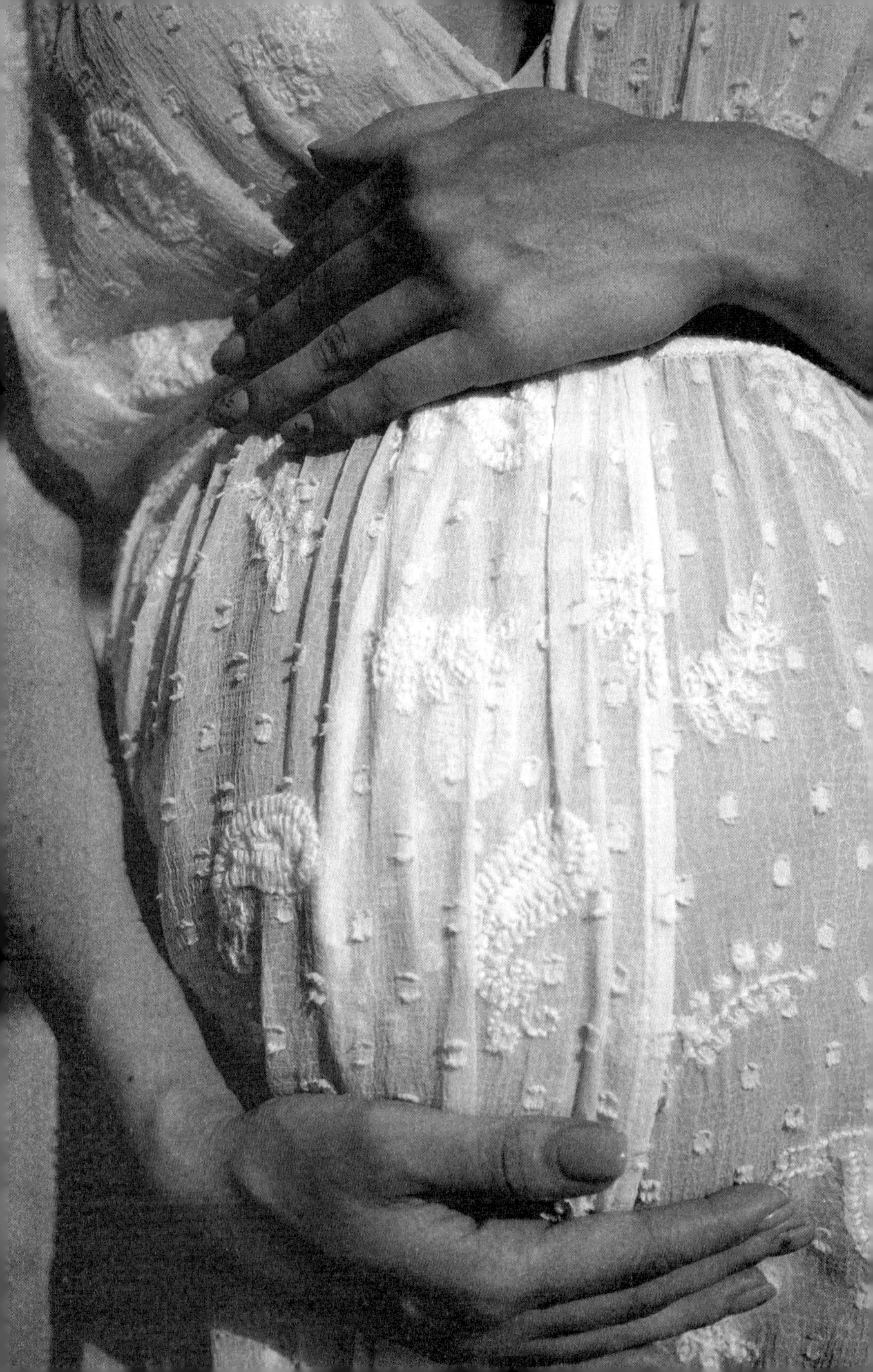

10

HERBS TO HELP YOUR PREGNANCY

Pregnancy is completely different for every single woman, but the one thing mothers all have in common is that this is a time of their lives that is beyond incredible in terms of what the mind and body are capable of. Whether you glide through it with the odd ache or find that you and your baby need a little herbal help, there are natural solutions for you.

The first thing you can start doing is increasing the amount and variety of fresh herbs you use in your cooking to get more vitamins and minerals. There is no need to check with your OB every time you add a bit of parsley or garlic to your food. That being said, discuss any concerns you have about using herbs or taking any other medications with your doctor or OB to be on the safe side. The same applies to those trying to get pregnant or breastfeeding.

Before looking into the herbs that can help you, I want to cover some that you should not use while pregnant.

HERBS NOT TO USE DURING PREGNANCY

First, don't use any essential oils, either topically or orally, because of their strength. Honestly, you probably have too much going on to find the time to patiently separate essen- tial oils, and we have plenty of safer options. Some herbs and spices, such as kava kava and ginseng, don't have enough research to understand their safe use during pregnancy.

Others are safe to use in a particular way or amount. For the culinary herbs, oregano and rosemary are safe in culinary amounts but shouldn't be drunk as tea as they could cause uterine contractions. *Aloe vera* is safe for the skin but shouldn't be taken orally because of the latex gel (The University of Texas at El Paso, n.d.).

The following list contains some herbs that may also induce uterine contractions:

- yarrow
- black cohosh
- blue cohosh
- chamomile
- gotu kola
- passionflower
- buckthorn
- feverfew

These are just a few herbs that possibly aren't safe during pregnancy. Double-check if you think there is an herb that can help you with specific problems. Now for the good herbs!

GINGER - ZINGIBER OFFICINALE

Morning sickness is one of the most common problems of pregnancy, especially during the first trimester. Gingerols, shogaols, and zingiberol are three active ingredients that can reduce morning sickness. These compounds also have anti- inflammatory properties, so you might be able to reduce the size of those swollen "cankles."

As the baby grows, your poor digestive system has less and less space. Ginger can help with digestive problems such as indigestion and bloating. Ginger root can help keep blood sugar levels regular and lower the risk of gestational diabetes. One study showed that six weeks of ginger tablets saw a significant reduction in fasting insulin in pregnant women (Hajimoosayi, et. al., 2020). It may also improve your circulation and blood supply to the baby!

PEPPERMINT

Peppermint tea is considered safer than other herbal teas because it lacks caffeine. It has been said that 1 or 2 cups of peppermint tea a day can help with nausea, heartburn, stomach upset, and headaches. While there hasn't been much research on peppermint and pregnancy specifically, the benefits have been passed down from generation to genera- tion, and the effects have been extrapolated from studies on other conditions. If you find the smell of peppermint relax- ing, you can make a lovely salve for massages.

LEMON BALM -MELISSA OFFICINALIS

Like peppermint, lemon balm tea hasn't been widely tested on pregnant women, but other research and personal experi- ences attest to its helpfulness. During the first trimester, the immune system is at its weakest, and lemon balm tea can give it a boost and prevent colds and flu. Lemon balm can also help calm nerves, irritability, anxiety and improve sleep.

MORINGA - MORINGA OLEIFERA

Now, this herb is one I would highly recommend for preg- nancy and breastfeeding, and the research supports this. Moringa is a plant native to India known as the drumstick tree or, more appropriately, the miracle tree because its benefits make it a superfood. We are going to talk about moringa in more detail in section three. For now, we will keep the focus on pregnancy.

Moringa can be a benefit to those trying to get pregnant. Moringa is high in various vitamins and minerals that can ensure you are in your best health before pregnancy begins. During pregnancy, moringa contains enough calcium and iron to meet the daily needed intake (Gopalakrishnan, et. al., 2016). It can also give you a natural energy boost if you miss your favorite caffeine drinks. Other benefits include massive amounts of vitamin A and seven times the amount of vitamin C in oranges. And for mothers who are breastfeed- ing, moringa can help increase milk production by double (Moringa Facts, 2017).

While all parts of the moringa plant can be used during pregnancy, it is best to use only the leaves. The leaves can be added whole to dishes or made into tea. Dried leaves can be ground into a powder and added to smoothies, soups, stews, curries, and so on.

So, the safest way to enjoy herbal remedies before, during, and after pregnancy is by drinking tea; the standard amount is 1 or 2 cups daily. A good idea is to vary the herbal teas you are drinking to take in the different benefits and reduce the risk of exposing yourself or the baby to excessive amounts of one particular active ingredient.

For the final chapter in this section, we are going to explore the all-important immune system and discover ways we can start preventing certain aliments rather than waiting to need a cure.

SINGLE

11

WHY YOUR IMMUNE SYSTEM IS SO IMPORTANT

When we talk about the immune system, we tend to think of colds and the flu; while this is part of it, it's only a fraction. According to Pfizer, a robust immune system can help reduce the risk of catching COVID-19 (Pfizer, n.d.). One of the common themes with herbs and superfoods is the high levels of anti-inflammatories. The immune system responds with inflammation when the body detects anything that doesn't belong, such as a virus or bacteria. A healthy immune system can create a barrier that protects the body.

Sometimes, one of these invaders that don't belong slips past the barrier, and the immune system cranks up its efforts to prevent it from multiplying. These systems have a tough job and could do with a helping hand from us to be as effective as possible. Lifestyle is important, but you can help your immune system with five special herbs.

BLACK ELDERBERRY – SAMBUCUS NIGRA

Black elderberry is native to Europe but now grows in many parts of the world. Though these other species will have significant benefits, the European black elderberry has the most benefits. Black elderberry contains vitamins A, C, and E and contains more antioxidants than other berries, such as cranberries and blueberries.

The key to its immune-boosting power is the polyphenols. These antioxidants, specifically anthocyanins and flavonoids give the berries a lovely dark purple color. Polyphenols can help the immune system by fighting free radicals that the body considers invaders, and Anthocyanins also have anti- inflammatory properties.

You can't eat black elderberries raw. The seeds inside contain cyanide-inducing glycoside, which can be toxic. The leaves and roots have the same toxin. To prepare black elder- berry, you always need to cook it. This isn't a problem because by simmering the berries in water for 45 minutes, you will have a decoction base for a syrup. This syrup can then be taken daily for immune support or up to a few times a day if you suffer from the flu or a cold. Drying the berries is another way to remove the toxins because cyanide evaporates. You can make a tincture with your dried berries or grind them into powder.

ECHINACEA – ECHINACEA PURPUREA

Even though I have a long history with echinacea, I forget how clever it is every once in a while. Two main ingredients are beneficial to the immune system, alkamides and polysac- charides. Alkamides stimulate the cells in the immune system, while polysaccharides help improves how the immune system works.

Echinacea helps cell activity in another way as well. The body has a set of cells called large granular lymphocytes (LGL), known as natural killer cells. They are part of the immune system and detect "bad cells" like those infected with a virus. These killer cells then destroy the infected cells. Echinacea can improve the activity of these killer cells.

Research is mixed on the benefits of echinacea. Still, one study found that the duration of a cold was shorter when drinking echinacea-based products compared to a placebo and no treatment (Barrett, et. al., 2010). Considering it has anti-inflammatory properties and pretty flowers, it's a wonderful addition to brighten your garden.

GINGER – ZINGIBER OFFICINALE

As we have seen the many benefits of ginger, I won't repeat what we have already learned. The anti-inflammatory and antioxidant properties of ginger can reduce harm to your immune system and help it function as it is supposed to. One study on chickens showed that 42 days of ginger powder significantly influenced the birds' immune responses; plus, the birds lost weight (Qorbanpour, et. al., 2018).

Ginger shots (a drink, not a needle!) are an excellent way to boost the immune system. This is because you can mix ginger juice with other immune-friendly ingredients such as lemon and honey.

GOLDENSEAL – HYDRASTIS CANADENSIS

Goldenseal is native to North America and was popular as an herbal remedy among Native Americans. Sadly, due to loss of habitat and overharvesting, wild goldenseal is not as abundant as it used to be. It's a member of the buttercup family, and the roots and leaves are used in herbal medicine.

Goldenseal contains berberine, an alkaloid with anti-inflam- matory, antibacterial, and antifungal properties. It is possible that berberine can block flu particles (Enkhtaivan, et. al, 2017) and help treat a cold. So far, most studies have been on animals, and scientists aren't sure if the same response would occur in humans. But for me, this is one of those herbs that we can rely on tradition while science catches up. Because of its active ingredients, goldenseal may also help with digestive problems, upper respiratory tract infractions, and allergies, so it is not just one for the immune system.

You will get the most health benefits from the roots. They can be used for teas and tinctures or dried and ground into a powder for cooking.

OREGANO - ORGANUM VULGARE

Oregano is one of those herbs you probably already have in your spice rack and will probably start sprinkling a little more generously from now on. Oregano's three main active ingredients are carvacrol, thymol, and rosmarinic acid. Carvacrol can stop the growth of bacteria, and rosmarinic acid is a powerful antioxidant. Thymol helps protect the immune system from toxins because it is antifungal.

Oregano essential oil has more antioxidants than other potent plants like St John's wort and blueberries. Studies have shown that the antibacterial properties in this oil can even be used against antibiotic-resistant strains of bacteria (Web MD, 2020). Therefore, it is an excellent choice for healing wounds and acne.

Although antioxidants and inflammation are throughout this book, particularly this section, we are only touching the surface, and these health topics go beyond helping the immune system. When we look at chronic illnesses, we will be able to appreciate the potential of herbs fully.

But for the final chapter in this section, we will learn how to relax because this is not only difficult but also something we sometimes feel guilty about doing. And it really shouldn't be this way.

12

STOP PUTTING OFF DE-STRESSING AND START RELAXING WITH YOUR PATIO POTIONS

I love technology, and there is no doubt that it has made our lives so much easier, especially in terms of commu- nication and keeping in touch with people. But (and it's a big BUT), technology has also swooped in and raised our stress levels sky-high. This has been seen even more since the pandemic.

Whether it was lockdowns or remote work, so many people (myself included for a while) became glued to one form of device or another. Work is no longer 9 to 5 because we have apps constantly ping to remind us of our responsibilities. Social media sites used to be filled with updates from friends and family, and now we can't scroll through without seeing some negative news.

We can't blame all our stress on technology. Generally speaking, life is much more fast-paced than it used to be, and it's rare for us to enjoy a walk in the park or just play with the children or grandchildren without feeling there is some- thing more pressing. And the thought of taking 5 or 10 minutes "just for you" is absurd.

We need to get better at de-stressing before it becomes chronic stress and causes more severe health conditions.

HOW TO USE YOUR LEFTOVER HARVEST TO RELAX

I am a huge fan of absolutely no waste wherever possible, and you probably already have an extensive list of herbs you want to grow. Before adding to that list, let's take advantage of some of the plants we have already discussed. Once you have become the master of your herb garden, your plants will likely give you so much to harvest that there will be some leftovers. Take the mint family, for example. It seems like I can take a plentiful harvest from my mint plant, and a couple of days later, it's like I never touched it.

Relaxing herbs that we have previously looked at include:

- chamomile
- lemon balm
- lavender
- peppermint
- valerian
- kava
- St John's wort

Another thing to remember is that any herb, spice, or flower you like the smell of will make you feel happier and relaxed. The smell of fresh basil always relaxes me because it reminds me of holidays and Italian restaurants. So, have faith in your nose when choosing leftover harvests to help you relax.

I used to love having many bubbles in my bath, but since so many products started to irritate my skin, I switched the bubbles to leaves, petals, and sprigs of herbs. I also like to make the most of my time at the computer, so you will often find a bowl of water under the table with my feet soaking up the benefits of some of my leftover herbs.

Aromatherapy is another great way to inhale health benefits and relax. You might think that you have to have some form of physical contact with an herb to take in the nutrients, but by inhaling, the benefits of an herb move quickly through the nose, through the lungs, and into the blood.

You can make aromatherapy candles if you have some left- over beeswax from a salve. If you use dried herbs and flow- ers, ensure none come into contact with the wick, as it could cause a fire. You can make potpourri by drying flowers and leaves and adding a few drops of essential oil or make a batch of decoction to use in diffusers around the home. Have fun and experiment with herbs that make you smile!

PASSIONFLOWER – PASSIFLORA INCARNATA

If you choose to grow passionflower, it will be hard not to sit in your garden for a few minutes and marvel at these flowers—a relaxing habit! The petals are fragile, almost like string, and start white in the center and turn purple, blue, or magenta on the outer edges. It's a climbing vine, so that you will need a wall or some kind of support. You will probably need to cover the passionflower in the winter because the frost can kill the plant.

Passionflower may help people to relax because it can increase the amounts of gamma-aminobutyric acid (GABA). GABA reduces brain activity, helping you relax and possibly even sleep better. If you have a stressful event coming up, using passionflower can help reduce anxiety. In one study, patients that were due for surgery took either passionflower or a placebo. The group that took passionflower reported significantly less anxiety (Movafegh, et. al., 2008). Neverthe- less, if you are scheduled for surgery, talk to your doctor before taking any form of passionflower. Although it isn't as potent as herbs like valerian or kava, it still may interact with sedatives and blood thinners.

ASHWAGANDHA – WITHANIA SOMNIFERA

Native to India, ashwagandha is one of the most important herbs in Ayurveda. Traditional root uses were a tonic, diuretic, astringent, stimulant, and even an aphrodisiac. The leaves are used to treat fever, and the flowers have similar effects as the roots. Even though it's native to India, you can grow ashwagandha from seeds in temperatures of about 70ºF.

Withaferin-A is one of the ingredients in ashwagandha that acts as an anti-stress agent. As an adaptogen, something that helps the body handle stress, it helps lower the activity in the body's system that regulates how we respond to stress.

Participants who took an 8-week dose of either 250 mg or 600mg of ashwagandha extract experienced lower levels of stress, lower cortisol levels, and improved sleep (Salve, et. al.,2019).

The roots contain the most withaferin, so for stress, you can use the roots to make teas, decoctions, syrups, and tinctures. For a better night's sleep, take your herbal remedy before bed. In Ayurvedic medicine, the leaves are also used. You can try grinding them up and adding them to warm water to drink on an empty stomach for a detox and possibly help with weight loss.

HOLY BASIL – OCIMUM TENUIFLORUM

Holy basil, also known as tulsi or the "queen of herbs," isn't the same as our regular basil, although growing the herbs is similar. Basil is sweeter, whereas holy basil has an intense peppery flavor but is typically used for its healing power rather than as a culinary herb. It's another herb with deep roots in Ayurvedic medicine and is native to India.

All parts of the plant have excellent nutritional value, including vitamins A and C, calcium, zinc, and iron. There are plenty of antioxidants as well as anti-inflammatory and antibacterial properties. The entire plant also acts as an adaptogen and can help overcome different types of stress, whether chemical, physical, emotional, or infectious. A study involving 33 participants taking 500 mg of holy basil extract twice daily reported the participants experienced less stress and anxiety and felt more social (Bhattacharyya, et. al., 2008).

There is no caffeine in holy basil, so it is safe to drink the tea daily. If the flavor isn't your favorite, this herb is also great in the form of a tincture.

Today, it doesn't matter if you are a housewife, husband, or a CEO, there is going to be stress. It's not selfish to take some crucial time to ensure you are looking after yourself. On the contrary, it's making sure that you are at your best to take care of those who rely on you.

A few years ago, I had a friend who had taken on the weight of the world—kids, full-time work, a sick parent, you name it. I knew giving her five different herbs would add more to her workload, and her exhausted brain couldn't cope with me waffling on about the benefits. I made a tincture with ginger, ashwagandha, and holy basil and asked her to bear with me and take a few drops each night. If you ask her now, she will tell you that just one tincture was enough to stop a complete breakdown from burnout and even enabled her to start enjoying life again after just a few weeks.

Unfortunately, not everyone can find herbal remedies before a more serious condition develops. Our final section will focus on those deeply concerned for their mental or physical health.

YOUR GOOD DEED OF THE DAY

Will you help me? I am so passionate about natural remedies and the power to grow our own medicine... right in our own backyards, window boxes and planters. Anyone can do this... but people won't hear about it without your help. **Please take 5 minutes to: write an honest review on Amazon.**

Your comments are the key to spreading the word and I would be grateful for your support. Just like natural remedies were passed down from family to family, generation to generation, your review will do the same! **Scan the QR code for a quick review!**

In the publishing world, for a book to be seen, it has to have reviews to be successful. And I want as many people as possible to know that they can grow, harvest and create powerful home remedies that will bolster their immunity and their health. Please help me to spread the power and the passion!

Thank you!

Jenni
Hello@homesteadmindset.com

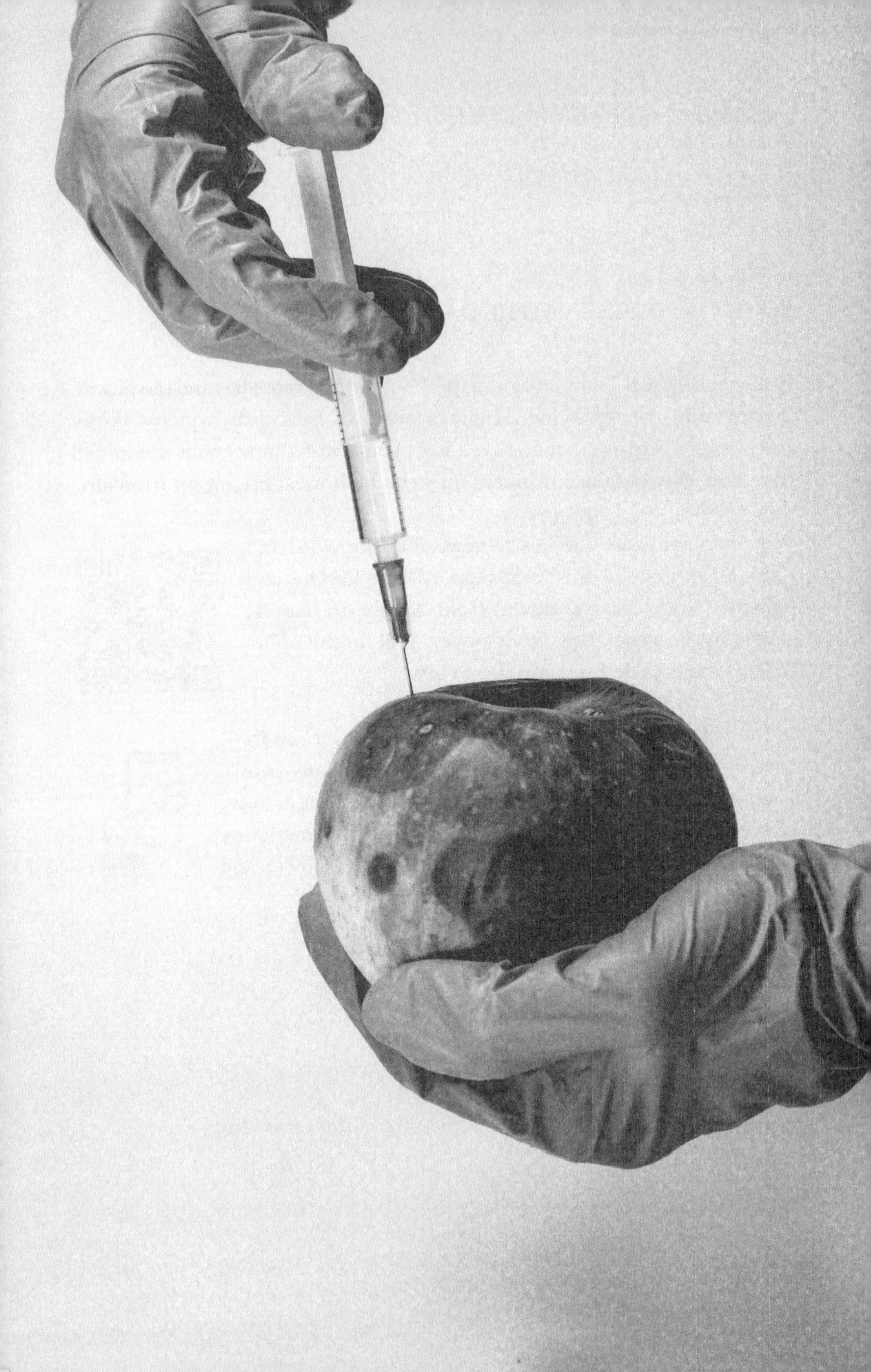

SECTION FOUR

HELPFUL HERBS FOR SERIOUS CONDITIONS

As their name implies, chronic diseases can't be cured—at least not yet! In 2020, researchers estimated that 24.9% of the US population would suffer from two or more chronic diseases and 48.3% would be chronically ill. This might not necessarily apply to you directly, but it could still impact your life if you have to take on the role of caregiver for a loved one. Taking care of a family member leads to an average of 20.4 hours of unpaid time, and many people have to cut back on their working hours to provide this care.

Chronic diseases cause seven out of ten deaths. As if that wasn't enough, 75 cents of every dollar spent on health care goes toward chronic diseases (The Silver Book, 2006). With the advances in science, it's now possible to understand how particular herbs can help manage symptoms, slow progres- sion, and even prevent some of these diseases. In this section, we will highlight some of the most prevalent chronic diseases and what you can start doing for yourself and your family immediately.

13

HEART DISEASE

Heart disease is an umbrella term for various conditions, some of which can be cured or controlled, and many can be prevented with a healthy life- style. Some heart conditions include diseases in the blood vessel, heart infections, abnormal heartbeats, diseases in the heart muscle, and problems with the valves. Some conditions can increase the risk of heart diseases, such as high blood pressure or high cholesterol.

It goes without saying that if you are concerned about your heart health, you must visit your doctor. And if you have a heart condition, discuss using some of the following herbs before trying them. For everyone else, don't delay growing these mighty plants for your heart health.

HAWTHORN - CRATAEGUS MONOGYNA

The small red berries of the hawthorn shrub contain several vitamin Bs, vitamin C, calcium, iron, and saponins—a compound that helps the body to absorb nutrients. The phenols and vitexin in the berries have anti-inflammatory properties, and vitexin also has anti-cancer properties. The antioxidants in hawthorn can help with heart disease, espe- cially the flavonoid rutin.

These active ingredients work as a heart tonic, improving the overall health of your heart. Hawthorn relaxes blood vessels so that blood can flow better and may help control high blood pressure. Some even believe that hawthorn extract can help people suffering from emotional matters of the heart.

The most popular herbal treats to make with hawthorn are tinctures and syrups. Hawthorn berries are toxic raw, so whatever you plan to make with your harvest, be sure to cook them first.

ROSE – ROSA CANINAE

Hawthorn and rose are from the same family, and some properties are similar. Roses contain vitamin C, iron, and calcium, with the added bonus of vitamins A and E. For heart health, the highest amounts of antioxidants are in the rose hips. They can improve circulation and strengthen capillaries. The rose petals are good for anti-inflammatory use and for improving your mood.

Rose tea and rose water are amazingly simple and effective. All you need to do is boil clean petals and inhale the tea while drinking it warm or leave the infusion to cool. Unlike other herbal teas, rose water can last in the fridge for up to 1 week. You can also dry the petals and grind them into a powder. The rose hips can be used for teas and syrups, but their flavor also makes them ideal for jellies and jams.

MOTHERWORT – LEONURUS CARDIACA

Motherwort is a prickly bush, and the small pink or purple flowers are almost furry. It doesn't have a particularly nice smell or flavor. Still, it has been used to treat heart disease for thousands of years. Motherwort is a member of the mint family and therefore is quite invasive. You may check with your local council or city hall before planting it, as some areas ban it for being so prolific.

Flavonoids, along with other antioxidants, can protect the heart. A small study involving 50 adults showed that moth- erwort extract could reduce a high heart rate by a small amount. Still, the most significant difference was a positive effect on high blood pressure, anxiety, and depression (Shikov, et. al. 2011).

Fresh flowers are ideal for tinctures. The leaves, flowers, and stems can also be dried for different long-term uses. For something different, you can make a vinaigrette with apple cider vinegar to add to salads.

LINDEN -TILIA

Linden trees are native across Europe and North America in temperate climates. Also called Tilia, many species of this tree can be grown in a container. The flowers and leaves are typically used for their medicinal benefits, but the flowers have more active ingredients and are sweet and smell lovely.

These flowers contain a good amount of vitamins, volatile oils, and antioxidants. The antioxidant quercetin is particu- larly useful for helping with inflammation in the cardiovas- cular system. The flowers often used dried in a tea can act as a vasodilator, causing a chemical reaction that dilates blood vessels, essentially lowering blood pressure.

GARLIC - ALLIUM SATIVUM

This superfood is back, and for good reason. We have seen how antioxidant-rich garlic is, so we only need to look at the proof. In a 2016 study, 88 people suffering from hyperten- sion (high blood pressure) took an aged garlic extract or placebo for 12 weeks. Results showed a drop in blood pressure and arterial stiffness (Ried, et. al., 2016).

The best way to increase your garlic intake is to infuse olive oil with garlic. Olive oil is rich in monounsaturated fatty acids that can also help lower the risk of heart disease.

CAYENNE - CAPSICUM ANNUUM

We are all familiar with the spicy red chilies, and it's hard to imagine that they are actually part of the same family as the potato and tomato. It's important to remember that you do need to use chili peppers, not bell peppers. The capsaicin that gives these little fruits their kick is what offers the health benefits, and there is no capsaicin in bell peppers.

Chilies are also packed with vitamins. One fresh pepper can have 72% of your daily vitamin C and 50% of the recom- mended vitamin A amounts! If you can't cope with the heat of fresh chilies, a teaspoon of dried powder can still have around 15% of the recommended daily vitamin A. The bene- fits boil down to the antioxidants and anti-inflammatory properties. One study showed that regular consumption of chili reduced the risk of heart disease by 13% (Chopan & Littenberg, 2017).

Chilies are super easy to grow; my grandkids can do it! Chilies are great for making a tincture and will spice up some of your cocktails too. You can also make a salve to help with aching muscles and joints.

BASIL - OCIMUM BASILICUM

There are over 60 types of basil, and many times, the name tells us more about the flavor. Just a few examples are lemon basil, mint basil, and one of the most common—sweet basil. Different types also have different active ingredients. Sweet basil has eugenol, and lemon basil contains limonene, both of which are antioxidants. The eugenol in sweet basil can block calcium channels and potentially lower blood pres- sure. Compounds in basil may also lower cholesterol, while magnesium can increase blood flow. Basil is easy to add to many dishes, but you can also try basil tea and infused oil.

GINGER – ZINGIBER OFFICINALE

Like garlic, ginger is known to us for its anti-inflammatory and antioxidant properties. It also has anti-platelet proper- ties that can help reduce the risk of blood clots. We don't know precisely how chemicals like gingerols and shogaols help to lower blood pressure and reduce heart disease, but a large, recent study showed promising results. Daily ginger consumption in a study involving 4,628 participants showed a decrease in high blood pressure and heart disease risk, and the greater the ginger intake, the lower the risks (Wang, et. al., 2016).

PARSLEY – PETROSELINUM CRISPUM

Parsley has a fresh, peppery taste, making it a highly versatile herb for the kitchen. It also vitamins A, C, B12, and K. Some of these antioxidants are water-soluble, making it easy to extract the benefits. Regular portions of parsley in your diet can increase your potassium levels and lower blood pressure. The high B vitamin folic acid levels help prevent oxidative stress affecting the blood vessels and the thickening of the artery walls. Another advantage of parsley is that it has antibacterial and anti-inflammatory properties!

THYME – THYMUS VULGARIS

I love the smell of thyme, especially if you are lucky enough to find wild thyme. Although it's a member of the mint family, the aroma and flavor are very different. There is so much nutritional value in thyme, including high levels of vitamins A, C, and K. It is also rich in potassium and antioxi- dants like thymol, lutein, apigenin, and thymonin. Thyme oil and thyme tea can promote cardio health allowing the veins and arteries to relax and lower blood pressure.

While these herbs can help with heart disease, there is another danger we need to be aware of. Heart disease is one of the most common causes of heart failure. Some herbs in our next chapter can also help with heart failure, but we will review more alternatives to lower the risk.

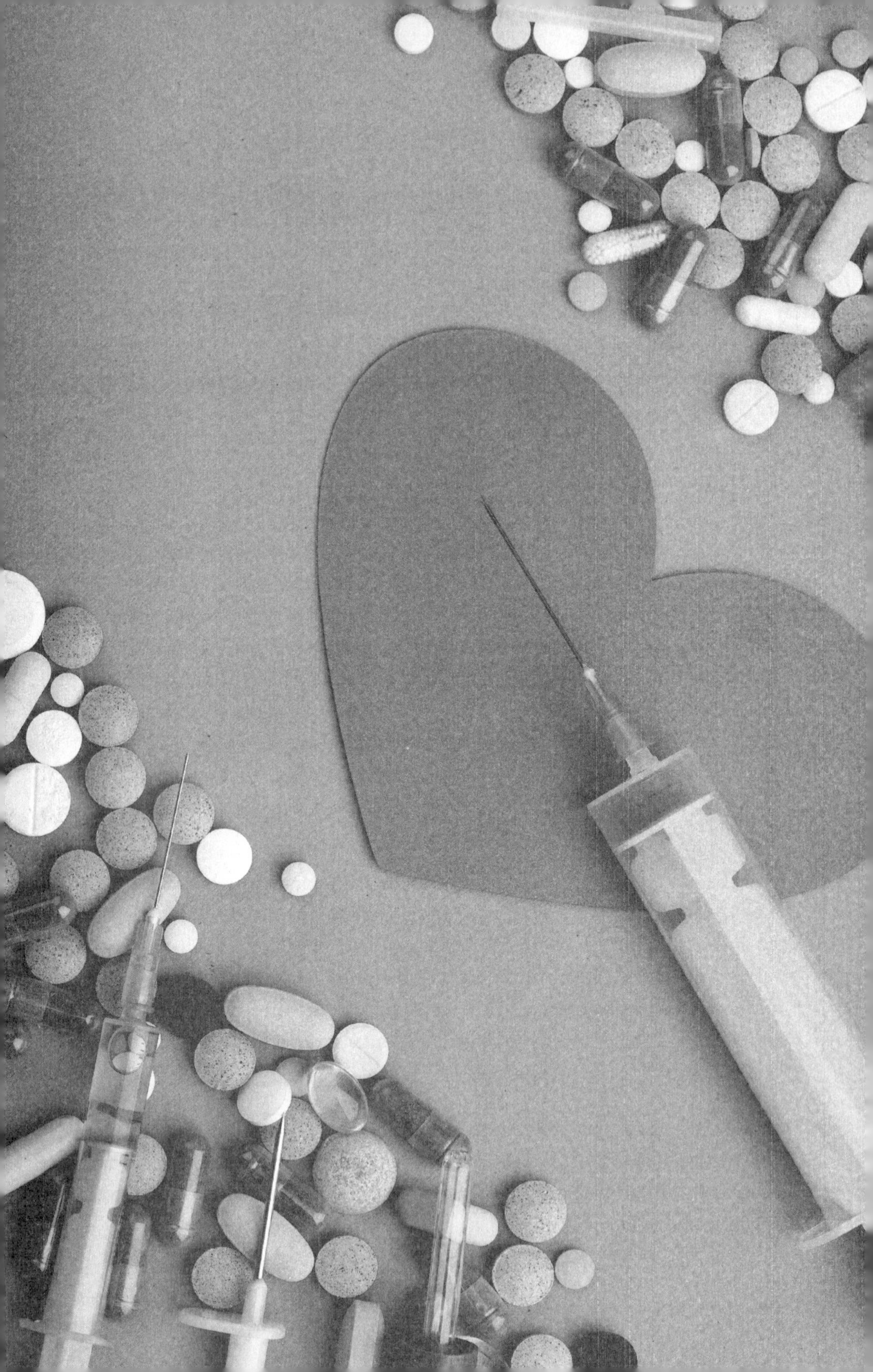

14

HEART FAILURE

Heart failure is technically a heart disease but deserves its own short chapter. This chronic and progressive disease is caused when the heart can't pump enough blood around the body. For the body to get enough oxygen, the heart has to compensate for this by enlarging, increasing muscle mass, or pumping faster. Causes of heart failure can be a heart attack (damaging the heart), high blood pressure, or cardiomyopathy (a disease of the heart muscle). All the herbs we discussed in the previous chapter help boost heart health and help prevent heart failure. We will revisit hawthorn for its specific use for heart failure as well as two other options.

HAWTHORN – CRATAEGUS MONOGYNA

Meta-analysis collected data from 13 trials and 632 patients with chronic heart failure. A treatment of hawthorn extract proved more beneficial than a placebo in several ways. Heart rate pressure decreased; dyspnea and fatigue, common symptoms of heart failure, improved, and there were few side effects (Pittler, et. al., 2003). More recent studies on rats have shown how hawthorn extract before a cardiac event can strengthen the heart and reduce the damage to tissues caused by a heart attack (Vijayan, et. al., 2012).

A typical dose for heart failure prevention is 80 to 300 mg of hawthorn extract two or three times a day. For tea, you should aim for 4 to 5 gm a day, and if you have made hawthorn jelly, aim for the same amount (Khalsa, 2021). It can take 4 to 5 weeks to notice an improvement in the physical symptoms.

Hawthorn has been referred to as the Swiss Army knife of heart herbs, and for a very good reason. If you are concerned about heart health or have a history of heart disease and heart failure in your family, keep this at the top of your list to grow.

TURMERIC – CURCUMA LONGA

It's the massive levels of powerful antioxidants in turmeric that might be able to prevent heart failure. In rats, curcumin doses helped make rats more resistant to heart failure than rats that didn't take curcumin. Inflammation was lower too. In the same studies, curcumin was able to reverse heart enlargement (Hitti, 2008).

More studies have been carried out since then, not just on animals. When 59 adults took either 50 or 200 mg of curcumin extract, it took just eight weeks to see an improve- ment in heart health. The 200 mg dose significantly improved, especially in the blood vessels (Oliver, et. al., 2016). Properties in turmeric may also reduce the frequency of heart attacks.

Regularly using turmeric in your cooking, teas, or tinctures promotes all-around heart health. This superfood can boost circulation, reduce the risk of blood clots, and help to heal the heart tissue. And guess what! It's also delicious and versatile.

GARLIC – ALLIUM SATIVUM

Even if you don't love garlic (even thought I do), your heart really does! Aside from the benefits, we saw for heart disease, such as lowering blood pressure and reducing the hardness of arteries, garlic may also prevent damage to the heart cells. The antioxidants in garlic have been proven to have cardio- vascular-protective properties. By increasing the natural killer cells, the heart is better able to fight free radicals and enable proper function. This is helped by the sulfur in garlic, which might lower heart tissue injury.

Because it is so versatile, there are plenty of ways to start adding more garlic to your diet. Rather than an apple a day, try to start living by the motto of a few garlic cloves a day. It's also a fun and easy plant to grow. Once you get started, you will have an abundance in your garden and probably never have to buy it again.

Herbs, spices, and certain berries have been well-docu- mented for their ability to promote heart health. That said, relying only on herbal remedies would be wrong. For certain heart conditions, you can't afford to risk switching prescribed medications for herbs. Still, you should speak to your doctor about which of these natural elements might work together with medication to improve the effectiveness.

Above all, neither herbal remedies nor medication should be relied on instead of a healthy lifestyle. Positive steps towards maintaining a healthy weight, keeping active, and reducing stress levels are key to preventing and managing conditions associated with heart disease. Fortunately, gardening can help with each of these!

Let's now move away from the heart discussions to focus on diabetes. Diabetes is another chronic disease in which we see a rise in alarming numbers. Your lifestyle can play a role in preventing and managing diabetes, but there are also some helpful herbs to look at in the next chapter.

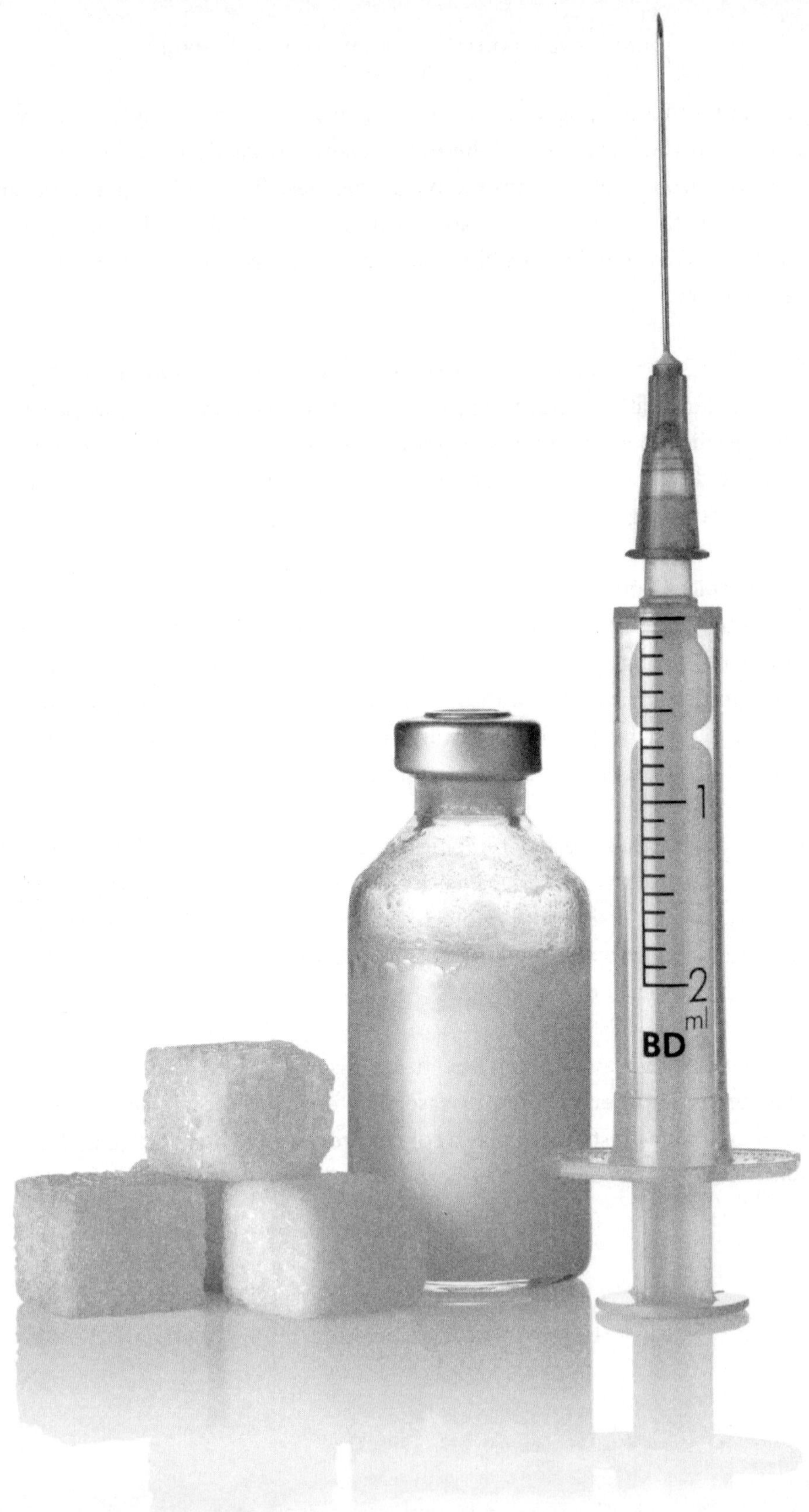
1
2
ml
BD

15

DIABETES

Diabetes is caused by how a person's body turns food into energy. Sugar or glucose is released into the bloodstream, and this increase in blood sugar tells the pancreas to release insulin. This insulin is essential because it allows blood sugar to enter cells to be used as energy. Aside from gestational diabetes, the two main types are type 1 and type 2. Type 1 diabetes is caused by the immune system not making insulin. Type 2, the more prevalent diabetes, is when the body doesn't use insulin as it should. The glucose remains in the bloodstream and may cause conditions like heart disease, complications in the liver, nerve damage and blindness.

Statistics are scary. There are 37.3 million adults in the US with diabetes (CDC, 2021), a number that has doubled in the last 20 years. Lifestyle changes such as weight control and physical activity can help with the symptoms, as can diet. So it is a worthy exercise to explore herbs that may help you manage your symptoms. It's worth mentioning that most studies on herbs have been on type-2 diabetes, but there are a couple herbs that may help with both types.

TURMERIC – CURCUMA LONGA

It all goes back to the fantastic curcumin that can help decrease the glucose in the blood. Studies on mice and rats have shown that curcumin reduces glycemia and hyperlipi- demia and can help with diabetes-related liver disorders (Zhang, et. al., 2013). Turmeric may also stabilize blood sugar levels, and research has been conducted on whether this superfood can prevent diabetes. It will be exciting to see what comes of human studies.

GINSENG – PANAX GINSENG

Ginseng has been tested on both animals and humans. The ginsenosides extracted from ginseng act as an anti-diabetic, helping with regulating the release of insulin and the use of glucose. Fasting blood glucose levels were lower after a 12- week study with 72 participants. Those taking an extract from ginseng berries saw a more significant drop than those taking an extract from the roots (Chen, et. al., 2019). The good news is that both American and Asian ginseng can help with type 2 diabetes.

Most studies have focused on ginseng supplements, but you can use the root to make teas and tinctures or add the powder to foods for a bitter flavor. Syrups aren't a good idea because of the sugar content.

CINNAMON – CINNAMOMUM VERUM

When I get a chance to bake, I just love cinnamon. The warm sweetness makes it a delicious addition to so many treats— even those suitable for people with diabetes. It wasn't till a few years ago that I considered growing it. It's surprisingly easy to grow if you are in hardiness zones 9 to 11, or you can grow it indoors too. The cinnamon plant is best kept in slightly dry soil with plenty of light. Once the plant starts to mature, you can harvest the stems and dry them to get the cinnamon sticks you would find in the store.

Studies are mixed on the benefits of cinnamon. Some volun- teers saw a 24% drop in blood sugar levels after taking 1 to 6 g of cinnamon for 40 days. Other studies showed no effect (Bruce, 2021).

Cinnamon may react with some medications, so check with your doctor first. Also, people with liver problems shouldn't take large doses. Aside from that, cinnamon is considered safe for most people. Try adding some cinnamon powder to your coffee, oatmeal, cakes, and pastries.

MILK THISTLE - SILYBUM MARIANUM

It's the antioxidant silymarin found in milk thistle that has hypoglycemic properties. It can lower blood sugar levels and may help the pancreas produce more insulin. Diabetic patients who took silymarin for 45 days saw a reduction in fasting blood sugar by 11% and blood insulin by 14% compared with the participants taking a placebo. Further- more, the participants experienced lower insulin resistance (cells ignoring insulin signals) and an increase in insulin sensitivity (the cell's response to insulin) (Rawson, 2021). Milk thistle may also help with liver conditions because of the silymarin.

You will want to use the seeds or the leaves to make a tea. Pop the whole milk thistle heads into a paper bag to dry for about a week. Give the bag a good shake to separate the seeds from the pods. Use the seeds in teas or baking, whole or ground into a powder.

HOLY BASIL - OCIMUM TENUIFLORUM

Holy basil is a solid option if you want to treat various symptoms of type 2 diabetes and prediabetes (a condition with high blood sugar levels but not high enough to be classed as type 2 diabetes). Symptoms include weight gain, high insulin levels, insulin resistance, high cholesterol, and hypertension. A meta-analysis looked at 24 studies on holy basil over the last five decades. One of these studies showed that 12 weeks of taking a 14 g decoction improved fasting glucose in 90% of participants (Jamshidi and Cohne, 2017).

There are so many ways to use holy basil. Fresh leaves make a lovely tea, and a tincture is easy to consume. For a sweet treat, try infusing honey with holy basil leaves.

FENUGREEK – TRIGONELLA FOENUM-GRAECUM

Fenugreek is an herb similar to clover, native to Europe and Asia. The plant contains flavonoids, alkaloids, and an impressive amount of iron. The chemical sotolon gives the leaves and seeds a maple syrup smell, although the flavor is somewhat bitter. Both the leaves and seeds are used in many cuisines, especially curries. It grows like most herbs, and as it has shallow roots, you won't need to worry about a deep container.

The good news about fenugreek is that it helps with type 1 and type 2 diabetes. Fenugreek seeds have high soluble fiber levels, delaying sugar absorption and modifying blood sugar levels. For type 1 diabetes, 100 g of seeds in a powder form reduced fasting blood glucose levels, and there was also an improvement in glucose tolerance. Similar effects were seen when people with type 2 diabetes took 15 g of powdered fenugreek seeds (Johanna, 2015).

Try using the leaves for teas and decoctions and in salads. Seeds can be roasted or dried and ground. As a spice, you can use it in soups and stews or make it into a paste to mari- nate meat.

ALOE VERA – ALOE BARBADENSIS

With its 75 different properties, it's not surprising that some active Aloe vera ingredients have antidiabetic properties. Just one tablespoon of *Aloe vera* juice for two weeks caused a reduction in blood sugar levels (Yongchiyudha, et.al, 1996). To help with type 1 diabetes, you should make a pulp out of the leaf instead of using the gel.

The other good thing about *Aloe vera* is that, as we have seen, it is excellent for the skin, used topically to help with skin wounds related to diabetes, like ulcers. It may also help with weight loss.

The best way to take all these herbs and spices for diabetes is orally, so now is an excellent time to experiment in the kitchen and increase your intake of these antidiabetics. Again, please check with your doctor first. Many studies include prescribed medications as well as the use of herbal extracts for the greatest effect.

The next chapter covers a subject that is very dear to me. With the shocking increase in prevalence, dementia has likely affected all our lives. You won't be able to cure your loved ones of dementia, but there are certainly ways to help and herbs that lower your risks.

16

DEMENTIA

As people age, it's relatively normal for the memory to start to slip. If we are honest, we have likely all walked into the kitchen to get something, only to forget what we were going for. (Surely, I can't be the only one!) That being said, dementia is not a normal part of aging and not something that we should assume we are all doomed to experience. Dementia is defined as a "deterioration in cogni- tive function beyond what might be expected from the usual consequences of biological aging," and globally, there are over 55 million people with dementia (WHO, 2021). With an aging population, it is estimated that by 2030, there could be as many as 78 million people with dementia.

The most common type of dementia is Alzheimer's, but there are other types, such as vascular dementia and dementia with Lewy bodies. Anyone who has seen the effects of dementia may find it hard to believe that herbs will help. It all goes back to those antioxidants! Once again, garlic, ginger, and turmeric may reduce the risk of dementia. Here are some other great choices.

LEMON BALM – MELISSA OFFICINALIS

While the antioxidants can help with inflammation, lemon balm also has rosmarinic acid that supports brain function. This herb can help to slow down plaque formation in the brain, which is linked to Alzheimer's. One study showed that lemon balm extract improved cognitive function in Alzheimer's patients aged 65 to 80 significantly more than a placebo (Akhondzadeh, et. al., 2003). The tincture used was 1 part lemon balm and 1 part 45% alcohol, and 60 drops were taken daily.

GOTU KOLA – CENTELLA ASIATICA

This special herb can work in more ways than one. First, it contains asiaticoside, molecules that can reduce cell death and boost free radicals. The antioxidants in gotu kola can improve mitochondrial dysfunction that causes neurodegen- eration. Finally, as a nervine adaptogen, extracts might help with memory function and intelligence. Studies on mice showed an improvement in memory, and in a small number of healthy adults, it resulted in better working memory and improved mood (Farooqui, et. al., 2018).

To use gotu kola to enhance brain function, you can use the leaves to make a tea or, better still, a strong decoction.

GINSENG – PANAX GINSENG

When it comes to taking care of your brain, it is best to choose the Asian variety of ginseng, as this is where most research has focused. Asian ginseng (also known by the Latin name *Panax ginseng*) has higher levels of ginsenosides than its American counterpart, making it more stimulating than its calming relative. These ginsenosides can increase the level of enzymes in the brain and have neuroprotective effects.

More recently, scientists have discovered a new active compound called gintonin, vital in reducing plaque build-up in the brain. More studies are needed, but combining ginsenosides and gintonin may enhance learning and memory (Kim, et. al., 2018). These two ingredients also help to fight oxidative stress. Teas, decoctions, and tinctures are the simplest ways to extract the brain benefits of Asian ginseng.

Siberian ginseng, also known as eleuthero, is also worth considering, although there is not enough evidence to support its use for dementia prevention. The roots contain a different set of active compounds called eleutherosides, and these chemicals may increase blood flow to the brain and mental alertness.

SAGE – SALVIA OFFICINALIS

Ah, our favorite Mediterranean culinary herb! Sage is easy to grow and easy to harvest. Plus, it makes a perfect addition to many different dishes. When healthy adults took a capsule of sage oil and were asked to perform a work recall test, they performed better than those who had taken the placebo. Early research also shows that sage might help prevent a breakdown in chemical messages and possibly serve as a treatment for Alzheimer's (University of Newcastle Upon Tyne, 2009).

Some types of sage contain thujone, a chemical that may cause seizures and liver damage with high doses. When used in cooking, there is no problem, but if you use teas and tinc- tures, it is best to stick to short-term use.

ROSEMARY – SALVIA ROSMARINUS

Of course, you can add rosemary to your culinary creations, but it is its use as aromatherapy that impacts brain function. If you are anything like me and have moments during the day when exhaustion hits you, just 3 minutes of inhaling rosemary essential oil can pick you up.

In one study, forty adults completed a math calculation. One group was given three minutes of lavender aromatherapy, and the other was given rosemary. The groups were then asked to do a math calculation again. The rosemary group was more alert and less anxious and could complete the calculation faster and more accurately (Diego, et. al., 1998).

MORINGA - MORINGA OLEIFERA

Where do we start with this little miracle plant? Moringa leaves have significant amounts of vitamins A, C, and D and several minerals. Add this to the alkaloids, tannins, and saponins. On top of that, moringa leaves are rich in antioxi- dants to fight free radicals and act as a nootropic (a drug used to improve memory and cognitive function).

Studies on rats showed that moringa leaf extract increased blood flow in the brain and dopaminergic system (how dopamine functions), which are critical for memory reten- tion. It also increased neuron density and decreased neurodegeneration. The results also showed that these positive impacts were more significant than in rats treated with Donepezil, a medication for some types of dementia (Suta- langka, et. al., 2013).

Moringa is now up there with turmeric for me. Try adding fresh, dried, or powdered leaves to meals and use fresh or dried leaves for a tincture. My latest choice is turmeric tea with a teaspoon of moringa to start the day!

The crucial takeaway from this chapter is that you shouldn't wait until the worst happens. It would take a pretty confi- dent person to say they wouldn't want a brain boost and a little extra mental clarity while helping prevent dementia in the future. Start adding these herbs and spices to your diet in any way you can, and remember that the more variety, the more benefits you get from each plant, not just for the brain. Don't forget that if you have stressed-out teens who are drowning in exams, they too might benefit from this chap- ter. If you happen to be caring for someone with dementia, the cure isn't in our reach yet, but you may be able to slow down the progress. If you notice that their dementia causes anxiety, consider options like lemon balm, gotu kola, and moringa, as they can help calm them too.

There have been a lot of studies in this chapter, and I felt it was necessary because of that "too good to be true" sensa- tion. The same can be said in the next chapter when we discuss herbs that can help with cancer.

17

CANCER

The big C word is one that many of us fear. There are more than 100 types of cancer, and the odds of getting cancer in your lifetime are alarmingly high. For females, it's a 1 in 2 chance for females, and for males, it's 1 in 3. Although, the odds of dying from cancer are much lower, 18.33% and 23.34%, respectively (American Cancer Society, 2021). Cancer occurs when cells in the body don't behave as they should. Instead of dying, cells grow abnor- mally and can then spread to other parts of the body.

There is no cure for cancer. There are treatments, thanks to modern science and technology. A cure would mean that cancer has been removed from the body and won't return. Complete remission means all cancerous cells aren't detectable, but not that all cells have been removed. Some herbs and spices can help to prevent cancer, and others might be able to change the way cells behave. Others can help manage symptoms.

I must reiterate here: no herb or spice will cure cancer. I don't want to be too repetitive, so remember plants like ginger, garlic, turmeric, rosemary, and moringa, with high levels of antioxidants, can help attack free radicals that damage cells. Let's take a look at some of the other inter- esting choices that are backed by science.

ALLSPICE - PIMENTA DIOCA

You wouldn't be alone in thinking that allspice is a combina- tion of other spices. This is because the flavor is like a mixture of cinnamon, nutmeg, and cloves. It actually comes from the berries of a tree. It is possible to grow allspice, but it's necessary to have the same climate as its native condi- tions—the Caribbean and Central America. If not, the plant may not produce fruit, but you can still use the leaves.

When mice with prostate cancer were injected or fed with allspice extract, cancer cells were destroyed. On top of this, the tumors' growth slowed by over 50% (Shamaladevi, et. al., 2013). Research attributed this to the powerful antioxidant quercetin, the compound ericifolin, and gallic acid, which all have cancer-fighting properties. There have also been promising results on other types of cancer.

If you are lucky enough to have a fruit-bearing allspice tree, dry the berries before grinding them into a powder. Increase your allspice intake by adding the powder to different meats as well as juices, cocktails, and of course, your eggnog.

BASIL - OCIMUM BASILICUM

Basil is packed with nutrients, and what interests us most here is beta-carotene—a carotenoid that converts into vitamin A in the body. Women who manage to take in healthy amounts of carotenoids can lower the risk of breast cancer. Basil oil also has a positive effect on leukemia and kidney cancer cells. The leaf extract can be highly effective in curbing the growth of lung tumors and lung, bladder, ovar- ian, and pancreatic cancer cells (Food for Breast Cancer, 2022), although studies were on mice.

You might be tempted to start using more powerful tech- niques to extract the benefits of basil. I don't recommend this because basil also contains heavy metals that may cause cancer. Basil oil is good, but a tincture might be too strong. Because it's such a good choice for cooking, stick to adding it to more meals.

CARAWAY - CARUM CARVI

The caraway plant produces pods of fruit that, when dried, people often mistake the spice as caraway seeds. It's the same plant, but they aren't seeds; they are dried fruit. Caraway has an earthy flavor that is a little bit bitter. It might remind you of coriander and anise. Caraway is rich in iron, zinc, calcium, and fiber. It also contains plenty of antioxidants, such as limonene and carvone.

Studies are limited, but the research shows that these high levels of antioxidants may help fight cancer. Caraway essen- tial oil was shown to significantly reduce the growth of colon cancer cells in rats (Kamaleeswari and Nalini, 2006).

You might want to add some ground caraway to sweet and savory baked goods. Sprinkle a little on roasted vegetables, or add it to your meat marinade. Caraway tea has long been a popular choice to help with digestion, and tinctures will work well when using dried fruit.

CARDAMOM - ELETTARIA CARDAMOMUM

Of all the different types of breast cancer, triple-negative breast cancer is the most difficult to treat and beat. Aside from the antioxidant cardamonin, cardamom has unique proteins that can help the immune system. One protein increases the body's ability to kill cancer cells, similar to how immunotherapy medications work. Animal studies have shown that cardamom has positively affected breast, cervi- cal, colon, gastric, ovarian, prostate, lung, leukemia, and melanomas (Ramchandani, et. al., 2020).

It's not one of the easiest plants to grow as it needs hot and humid climates. You will need temperatures of 64°F to 95°F and humidity levels of around

75%. The seeds in the pods can be dried and used whole or ground. You can use cardamom much like you can caraway, and a teaspoon of ground cardamom in with your ground coffee beans adds a lovely aroma to your morning brew!

CINNAMON – CINNAMOMUM VERUM

Researchers have used hot water extraction of cinnamon to treat male mice with melanoma cells. The mice were treated with cinnamon extract for 30 days. The growth of the tumors was significantly inhibited, and a difference in the growth rate was observed in as little as 48 hours (Kwon, et. al., 2010). Cinnamon pairs well with cardamom to help increase the intake.

CIL ANTRO – CORIANDRUM SATIVUM

There have been plenty of studies on cilantro's health bene- fits, but the first one related to cancer was in 2013. Scientists took leaves, stems, and roots from the plant and extracted active ingredients with water and alcohol to determine which parts had the higher amounts of antioxidants. The roots and alcohol extract came out on top.

The extract contains ascorbic acid, which has both antioxi- dant and anticancer properties. The same extract led to "apoptosis," a process that removes unwanted and extremely damaged cells. It can also reduce H2O2, a chemical that produces radicals that can lead to DNA damage (Tang, et. al., 2013).

Don't abandon the leaves and keep adding them to your culi- nary creations, but later, we will look at how to harvest the roots of perennial plants so that you can make your own tincture.

BLACK CUMIN – ELWENDIA PERSICA

Before looking at the health benefits of black cumin, it's important to know our species because it's not the same as cumin. In fact, it's not even in the same family. Cumin is a member of the parsley family; black cumin is in the buttercup family. It is also known as black seed, black caraway, Roman coriander, and nutmeg flower. To check if you have the right plant, look for the Latin name *Nigella sativa.*

There are mixed opinions on black cumin. Some research shows no effects on cancer cells. However, black cumin is approximately 30% thymoquinone (Alkhatib, et. al., 2020). This active ingredient has antioxidant, radioprotective, and chemopreventive properties. This spice may reduce the side effects of chemotherapy and enhance the effectiveness of medications and radiotherapy.

What is confirmed is that black cumin is high in antioxi- dants, so have a go at using the seeds as you would black pepper.

THYME AND OREGANO

These two herbs contain thymol, carvacrol, and thymohdro- quinone, which have anti-inflammatory, antibacterial, and antioxidant properties. They're also the ingredients that give these herbs their flavor. It's the thymohdroquinone that has anti-cancer properties.

The downside is that adding thyme and oregano to your food won't be enough. Biochemists are now looking at ways to increase or synthesize this anti-cancer compound. Until then, keep adding these herbs to your food. Consider making a tincture with a higher alcohol percentage to extract more benefits.

PARSLEY AND DILL

Unlike thyme and oregano, which have the same beneficial properties, parsley and dill must be used together. When parsley and dill seeds are combined, they produce glazio- vianin A. Glaziovianin A is a compound that works like an antimitotic—a drug that prevents cell division and, there- fore, cell growth. This compound is nothing new. You can get the same effects from Brazilian tree leaves, but this is an expensive process. Conversely, both parsley and dill are cheap and easy to grow. In fact, they are currently booming in my garden right now!

Scientists highlighted the prevention of cell growth by testing glaziovianin A on the embryos of sea urchins. The findings were then confirmed by using human lung, prostate, breast, ovarian, and colon cancer cells, as well as melanomas (Moscow Institute of Physics and Technology, 2016). Knowing this isn't only exciting for the future of cancer treatments but also gave me more inspiration on how to use these herbs. Typically, I would have only used the leaves, but now I like experimenting with the seeds to make infused oils and tinctures and then extracting the essential oils.

There is more good news when it comes to herbs and fighting cancer. Treatments such as chemotherapy can have some nasty side effects. On the other hand, herbs have very few side effects and are a less toxic way of helping treat cancer. I would never recommend someone stops cancer treatment and use an all-herbal treatment. Although you can see how deep my love for herbs goes, no layperson should recommend this. Speak to your doctor about how best to use herbs, and definitely start adding more of these delights to your food.

I understand that the last two chapters have been a little intense, and though we are still in the section on chronic conditions, the next chapter will explore herbs that help with two chronic illnesses that aren't life-threatening but do impact the quality of life.

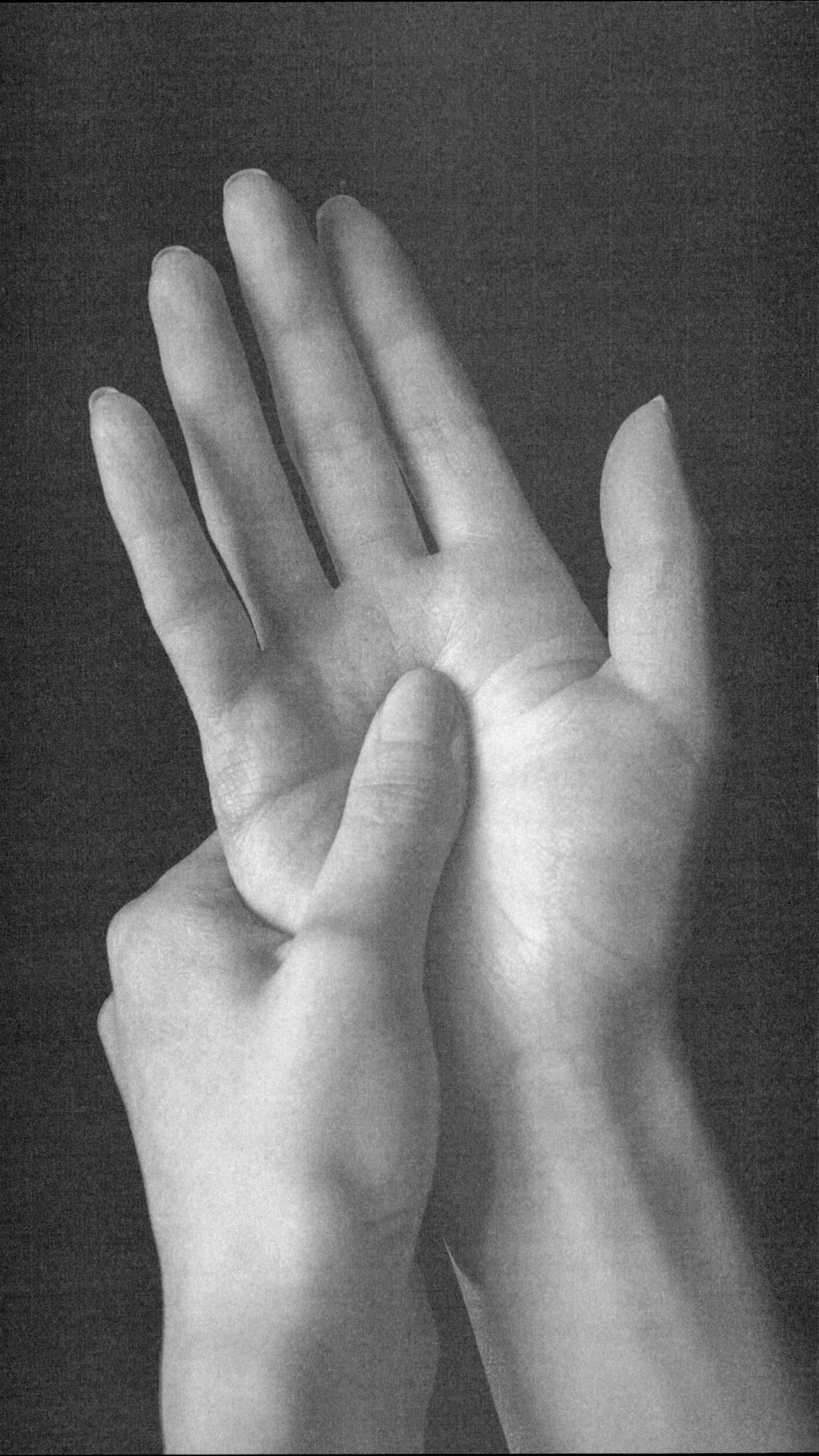

18

ARTHRITIS AND OSTEOPOROSIS

Arthritis and osteoporosis are both associated with older age, but it's worth knowing that environment and genetics may increase the risk factors. Arthritis is a swelling in the joints, often with pain and stiffness. It's diffi- cult to know precisely how prevalent osteoporosis is because the symptoms are far less noticeable. Many people don't realize they have low bone density until they break a bone, which is why it is sometimes called a "silent" illness. You can also have both at the same time!

We are going to look at two categories of herbs in this chap- ter. One will cover herbs and spices that can help with bone mass. Then, we will look at herbs that can help with joint pain and swelling. There will be some of those anti-inflam- matory properties that are so beneficial for us. The goal is to manage symptoms so people can have a better quality of life.

RED SAGE – SALVIA MILTIORRHIZA

Red sage is a beautiful perennial that requires a long growing season. It's best to start your seeds indoors. These seeds need soil that is rich in nutrients and not too wet. The plant, also called danshen, is popular in Traditional Chinese Medicine. The roots contain the most benefits for bones as well as heart and liver health.

Vitamin K found in red sage is essential for bone metabolism, the cycle of bone growth and resorption. It also contains tanshinones and magnesium lithopsoermate B, which can help bones. Salvianolic acid is another compound that helps bones and has anti-inflammatory properties. Studies have shown that red sage can improve bone mass density and reduce pain (Guo, et. al., 2014). Although the number of participants noticing a positive effect was high, the duration and size of the trials were limited.

Use the dried roots to make teas and tinctures. You may prefer a tincture to a tea, as the flavor is quite bitter. Also, as the studies have looked at short-term use, there isn't enough evidence on the long-term use of red sage, so it's a good idea to stick to just a couple of months' use to be cautious.

RED CLOVER – TRIFOLIUM PRATENSE

Red clover is another perennial, but in this case, the flowers are typically dried and used for medicinal purposes. It is native to Europe and Asia, but you may find it growing in meadows in North America. Research is mixed, but there could be a good reason for this. Some studies have shown no benefits, but for menopausal women, red clover may help.

The flowers contain calcium, magnesium, phosphorus, potassium, and vitamin C. More importantly, they have high levels of isoflavones, chemicals that act like estrogen, which drops during menopause. After 12 weeks of taking red clover extract, menopausal women had improved bone health, whereas women taking a placebo experienced a decline in bone mass density (Thorup, et. al., 2015).

Aside from teas and tinctures, you can infuse the oil and make a salve to use red clover topically.

THYME – THYMUS VULGARIS

Aside from antioxidants, thyme has many nutrients that boost bone health, such as vitamin K, calcium, magnesium, manganese, and zinc.

Postmenopausal women taking a 500 g thyme supplement twice a day saw a significant increase in bone mass density compared with a similar group taking a calcium and vitamin D supplement (Raghif, 2015).

TURMERIC - CURCUMA LONGA

Once again, the curcumin in turmeric is our hero - it has even been proven to improve bone density. One study compared the bone density of people over 70 years old taking a daily turmeric supplement. Bone density in the heels, jaw, and fingers improved by 7% (ChemDiv, 2017). With the added benefit of boosting brain function, turmeric is a sensible choice for the elderly. Remember that turmeric isn't easily absorbed and should always be paired with black pepper.

With its anti-inflammatory properties, turmeric can also help with swollen joints and pain caused by arthritis. If you have leftover infused oil, melt some beeswax to create a salve to rub onto joints.

BORAGE - BORAGO OFFICINALIS

You will want to collect the seeds from these pretty little flowers. The seeds have high levels of gamma-linolenic acid, an omega-6 fatty acid that helps to keep joints working as they should. Add some flowers to your cooking but save the seeds to create infused oil. Use the oil topically for personal use, but for culinary purposes, add it to recipes that don't require cooking.

EUCALYPTUS - EUCALYPTUS OBIQUA

Eucalyptus is a good option for pain management due to its flavonoids, anti-inflammatory properties, and analgesic properties. Many over-the-counter pain relief creams contain eucalyptus essential oil. Use the leaves to make an infused oil that can be added to baths or used as a massage ointment. If you extract the essential oils, a few drops can be added to the bath, but don't forget to dilute it before using it topically. Inhaling eucalyptus essential oil may also help relieve pain.

ALOE VERA – ALOE BARBADENSIS

As we saw previously, Aloe vera has 75 active ingredients. Antioxidants will help with the free radicals, but the anti- inflammatory C-glucosyl chromone is found in the gel and might relieve your short-term pain when rubbed straight onto the joints. The juice from the outer leaves contains minerals that may help with chronic pain.

CINNAMON – CINNAMOMUM VERUM

Flavonoid compounds and antioxidants such as catechin and procyanidin are some of the most potent components that make cinnamon an excellent anti-inflammatory. One study examined how cinnamon affected eight inflammatory markers in women with rheumatoid arthritis. Many of these markers were significantly lower in women who took 500 g of cinnamon powder daily for eight weeks (Shishehbor, et. al., 2017).

CAT'S CLAW – MARTYNIA ANNUA

Cat's claw is a vine that grows in the Amazon and Central America. It has impressive climbing abilities and will even grow on surfaces like glass. The underground tubers spread without seeing them, so think about growing cat's claw in a container if you don't want more popping up in the garden.

The anti-inflammatory properties in cat's claw are tannins and sterols. People who took 60 mg of cat's claw with their rheumatoid arthritis medication saw a 29% reduction in the number of painful joints (Mur, et. al., 2002). It would be nice to see more extensive studies, but it's still a good result.

The roots and bark are used for their anti-inflammatory benefits, and one of the most popular methods is to dry the parts and use them to make tea. You can also try grinding the dried parts into a powder and adding the powder to coffees and smoothies.

CAYENNE - CAPSICUM ANNUUM

Cayenne is probably one of my favorite choices for topical pain relief because I love the heat that comes from capsaicin. It works by reducing a chemical that carries pain messages to the brain. Rheumatoid arthritis patients used a cream containing 0.025% capsaicin four times a day for four weeks, and Osteoarthritis patients did the same. Rheumatoid arthritis patients felt an average of 57% less pain, and osteoarthritis patients had a 33% reduction in pain (Deal, et. al., 1991).

Please don't forget the importance of a healthy lifestyle when it comes to both arthritis and osteoporosis. It might feel like the last thing you want to do when your joints are aching, but exercise will help. Herbs should be there as a support, not the solution.

Chronic pain can also lead to depression. Those who suffer from arthritis have more than double the risk of experi- encing symptoms of depression (CDC, 2021). The last few years have pushed many of us to our limits, and anxiety and depression cannot be ignored. When tension takes over your life, it's time to incorporate herbs into your life before the problem gets out of hand.

19

DEPRESSION

Despite all that we have been through, especially during the pandemic, it still shocks me that mental health is still such a taboo subject. Between lockdowns, homeschooling, remote work, and the horrendous number of deaths, stress, anxiety, depression became the new norm. Stressful moments are a given part of life. Depression isn't.

The truth is there is a spectrum of depression. Many people walk about their daily lives almost in a zombie state, just putting one foot in front of the other. They may not be clini- cally diagnosed with depression but struggle just the same. Others can't find the strength to get out of bed, and there is certainly no shame in that. Only you can decide if you need to see a doctor or speak to a professional. Some herbs have been proven to help boost mood and depression, but if you remember what we said in the beginning, each person is different, and every herb will have a different impact. Give herbs time to have an effect, keep track of any changes in your feelings, and talk to doctors about alternative herbal options that are safe to use with other medications if necessary.

KAVA KAVA – PIPER METHYSTICUM

The roots of kava have 18 kavalactones that are mood-alter- ing, but scientists haven't been able to pinpoint precisely which one does what.

Kava may help you sleep, and many of us know that insomnia doesn't help when you aren't feeling yourself. It may also help reduce anxiety. One Australian study showed that kava root extract positively impacted people who suffered from general anxiety disorder (Sarris, et. al., 2011).

Because research is limited, kava is an herb that you should only use for short-term periods. There are fewer side effects than many over-the-counter treatments, but you should be aware that drowsiness is an effect. A wise use would be as tea before bed.

GINKGO – GINKGO BILOBA

Anti-inflammatories and antioxidants can help with anxiety and depression. This might be because these properties help the body cope with stress hormones. Studies on mice showed that ginkgo before a stressful situation reduced the emotional impact of the stress (Montes, et. al., 2015). Some women find that ginkgo can help with irritability and premenstrual syndrome. Use the ginkgo leaves to make teas, decoctions, and tinctures for daily use.

BRAHMI – BACOPA MONNIERI

This herb can sometimes be confused with other ground cover crops because of its creeping nature. It has numerous small leaves with white and occasionally purple flowers. Although it is native to India, it now grows in wetlands across all continents.

Brahmi is popular in Ayurvedic medicine as a brain tonic, and traditionally it was used for its ability to improve inspi- ration. It has also been used to help people connect with their spiritual nature and enhance spiritual practices like yoga and meditation.

Science tells us that brahmi is adaptogenic and helps the body cope with stress. It can lower cortisol levels and improve mood. After 12 weeks of taking 300 mg daily, participants in one study had lower anxiety and depression scores than those taking a placebo (Calabrese, et. al., 2008).

The abundance of leaves will give you plenty to make teas and decoctions, which can be dried to make a powder for smoothies and cooking. You can also make juice from the leaves to appreciate the bitter-sweet flavors.

PASSIONFLOWER – PASSIFLORA INCARNATA

The stems, flowers, and leaves can be used to help with insomnia, anxiety, and depression. It is thought that passion- flower extract can increase the amount of gamma-aminobu- tyric acid in the brain. GABA reduces brain activity, so instead of your mind spinning out of control, you might be able to relax more. A meta-analysis examining nine studies on passionflower showed that most people felt less anxious and had no adverse side effects (Janda, et. al., 2020).

As with many of the herbs in this chapter, a tea or tincture is the best use, typically before bedtime.

VALERIAN – VALERIANA OFFICINALIS

The use of valerian to help insomnia dates back to the ancient Greeks. There has been plenty of research, but nothing concrete on valerian's effectiveness on depression, and some of the studies were considered weak and unreli- able. Other research examined valerian in conjunction with other herbs, so it's unclear which herbs had the most signifi- cant effect. Research has shown valerian root reduces brain activity and changes how brain waves respond to stress and anxiety (Summer, 2022).

Although the evidence is weak, valerian root tea before bed can help with sleep, and for some, may help with anxiety and depression.

ST. JOHN' S WORT – HYPERICUM PERFORATUM

St John's wort is a popular choice for treating depression because it can be as effective as selective serotonin reuptake inhibitors (SSRIs) but without the side effects that often come with antidepressants. Scientists are still looking into how the plant works. The hypericin, hyperforin, and flavonoids could be responsible for increasing happy hormone levels in the brain. It might also help with related conditions such as seasonal affective disorder and obsessive- compulsive disorder.

Use the flowers and leaves to make teas and tinctures, but expect 3 to 6 weeks before depression ease. A tincture using fresh flowers may have the most benefits. St. John's wort is suitable for mild to moderate depression. For severe depres- sion, you should talk to your doctor.

BLACK COHOSH – HYPERCUM PERFORATUM

Black cohosh has long stems with tons of small white flow- ers, making it easy to spot in the woodlands of North Amer- ica. The roots contain the medicinal properties. Black cohosh alone isn't known for its antidepressant abilities. This is an excellent herb for menopause and the wide range of physical symptoms. You may not have heard of menopausal depression. Black cohosh may help lift a depressed mood as well as reduce hot flashes and the anxiety that comes with them. Use the roots for teas and tinctures.

Too many people with anxiety and depression go through life without treatment. Whether that's because of the stigma of seeking treatment or accepting that life is just this way, it's not something anyone should have to live with. Interestingly, no new pharmaceutical therapies have been released in the last 25 years. This is one area where we should rely more on herbs and "forget the pharmacy" to avoid the side effects of SSRIs.

As this section ends, we have covered herbs that can help you and your family—from cuts and bruises to caring for your heart and brain. The only thing left is to get out in the garden and plant some of these fantastic treats. Regardless of your gardening skills, you can grow anything as long as you pay close attention to the first step!

SECTION FIVE

GROWING YOUR HERBAL GARDEN

"We may think we are nurturing our gar•en, but of course our gar•en is nurturing us."

— JENNY UGLOW

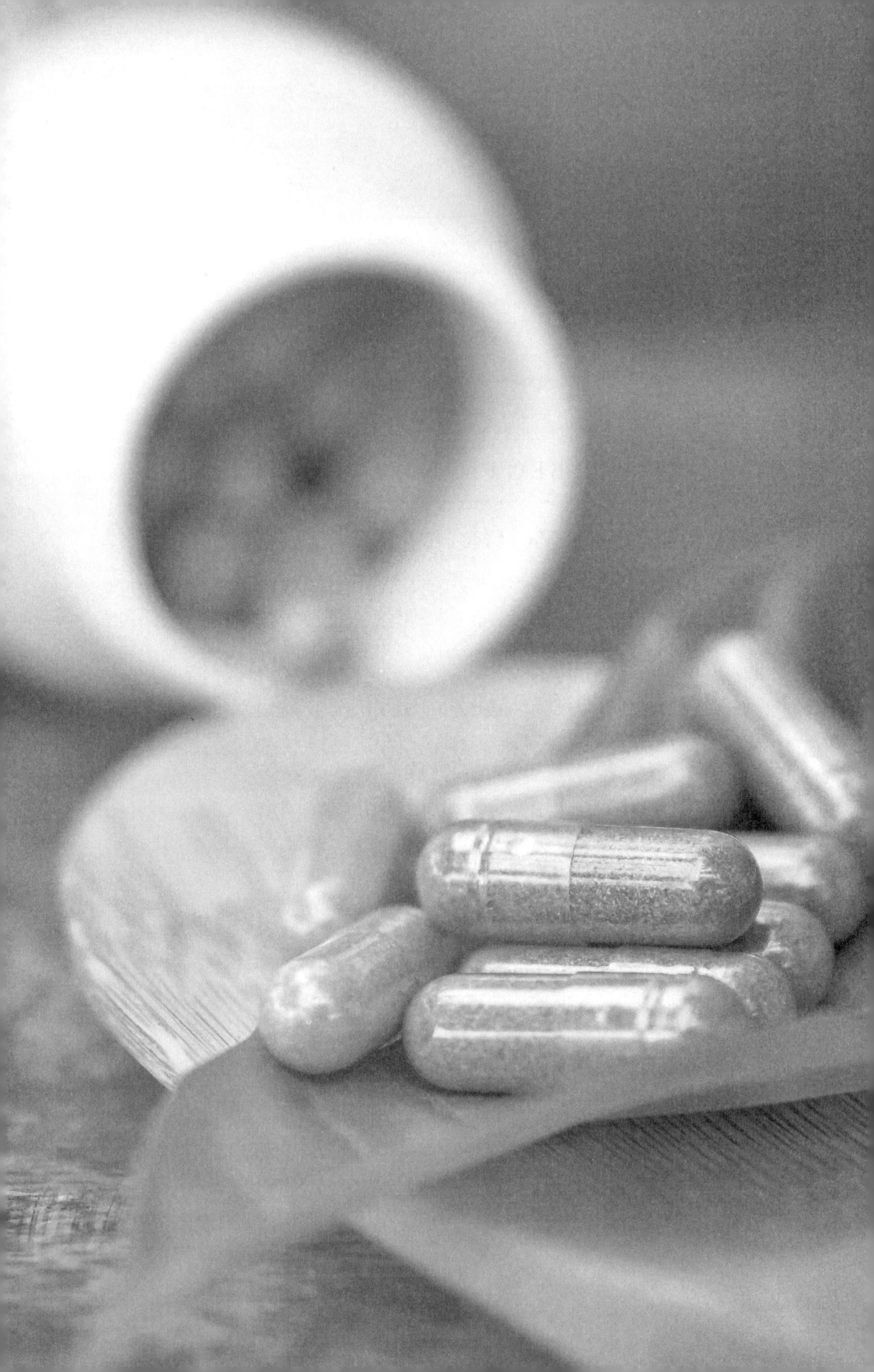

20

5 STEPS TO SAYING GOODBYE TO YOUR PHARMACY

Finally, it's time to get into the garden! By now, you should have an idea of some of the herbs and spices you want to grow. I started my herbal garden years ago, so it's normal that I have had time to add more elements each year. I started with just a few simple culinary herbs while learning the ins and outs of growing things from seeds. You can grow anything - I promise. Half of successful gardening is knowledge, and the other, more difficult half is patience.

Every gardener reaches a moment when they question their own abilities. Perhaps your seeds don't germinate, so you go straight for the nursery starts (baby plants grown by the local nursery), but you manage to kill those, despite watering them every day! You even spoke kindly to them! What more could they need?

In this hands-on chapter, we will look at five simple (I prom- ise) steps to grow your herbs and spices. Even more impor- tant is growing healthy and robust plants to provide the most benefits. For step one, grab a piece of paper and a pencil as we learn how to prepare your herb garden.

STEP 1 : PREPARING YOUR HERB GARDEN

How much space do you have for your herb garden? It's normal to have read all the previous chapters and imagine that you will never have the space for all you want to grow. For now, the focus should be on three or four of your favorite herbs and spices. Start your herb garden even if you only have a windowsill. The important part is to start!

Other ideas for smaller spaces include vertical hanging systems. With two bits of long cord, you can attach various containers that hang in one spot. Think about recycling soda bottles, food cans, and other containers. Take advantage of as much outdoor wall space with hanging baskets. If you have an old ladder, use the steps to place pots for a vertical herb garden.

If you have herbs with the same growing conditions, you can use one terracotta herb planter with several holes. Each herb can be grown from a different spot, saving tons of space.

For larger gardens, raised beds are a popular choice. You will have more control over soil health, and you can create a deep enough bed for your planting needs. If your garden is already well established, think about planting herbs along the borders for easy access.

Speaking of soil, plant beds are much like our own beds as every person has their personal definition of comfortable. Not all plants require the same soil conditions, specifically soil type and pH. Understanding your soil type is worth taking some time before directly sowing anything into the ground. Make the necessary adjustments so that your soil has the perfect level of nutrients. You might see websites suggesting you feed your herbs with fertilizer. I wouldn't go down this route. Fertilizers encourage rapid growth but don't give the plants the necessary time to develop all their health benefits.

If you need to add nutrients to the soil, make your own compost. While there are many compost systems, all you need is a large plastic garbage can with holes around all the sides and the base. Place the can on some bricks so the air can circulate from the sides and the base. Then, start adding your kitchen scraps. Compost needs three things: a mixture of greens and browns, air, and water. So aside from kitchen scraps, you should compost dried leaves and fresh lawn cuttings (your green). The compost also needs air, so shake the can occasionally, and finally, it needs water. Things not to add to the compost include meat and oils and don't compost anything you have pruned that might be diseased. Creating your compost allows you to reduce household waste and feed your plants seriously.

The next thing to consider for your planning is the amount of sun your herb garden will receive. Most herbs do well with full sun, meaning more than 6 hours of sunlight daily. Cilantro, mint, tarragon, and thyme are a few of the excep- tions that do better in partial sun. Check the seed packet to know whether your choices need full or partial shade.

Finally, knowing your hardiness zone is essential. You can look it up in google if you don't already know. The hardiness zones give you an idea of the minimum temperatures a plant can handle. The zones range from 1 to 13, with one being the coldest and 13 being the hottest. Each zone is further separated into a and b. These zones are helpful, especially if you are a beginner, but they shouldn't be the only thing you refer to when choosing your herbs. The zones don't consider rainfall, wind, humidity, or sunlight, which all impact grow- ing. The coldest temperatures won't apply if you plan to bring your plants indoors over winter.

STEP 2 : PL ANTING HERB SEEDS AND SPICES

The first thing to always check is the seed packet to confirm the specific needs. With thousands of plants, it's impossible to list how to plant each one. We will look at the general tips for growing herbs, spices, and flowers. The packet informa- tion will increase the chances of germination.

Don't feel compelled to go out and buy starter pots and pods. Egg cartons and toilet rolls work just as well, if not better.

When it comes to transplanting, the cardboard can be planted in the ground and will add more nutrients as it degrades. It gives the delicate roots some extra protection too. The one thing you should always use is fresh potting soil.

Herbs can be started indoors 6 to 8 weeks before the last frost. To start the seeds outdoors, ensure the last frost has passed. Sprinkle 2 or 3 seeds in each starting pot, and then sprinkle some soil on top. You only need the seeds to be around ¼ of an inch under the soil so that plenty of light can get to them and germination can occur. Use a mister to keep the soil moist.

Flowers can be a little more complicated, depending on whether it's an annual or perennial. Annuals have a one- season life cycle, whereas your perennials will last for a few years. Annuals can be hardy or tender, and the names give you a clue. Hardy plants are tough enough to cope with winter and should be planted in late fall or early winter. Tenders should be planted in late spring, around six weeks after the last frost. Examples of tender herbs are mint, chives, dill, basil, parsley, cilantro, and tarragon, because of their tender stems & leaves. Plant perennials in the early fall unless winters are harsh. Then, plant in the spring after the last frost. Look at the width of each seed and plant the seed 2 or 3 times the width of the seed apart.

Beneficial roots, such as garlic, ginger, and turmeric, may take a few months to mature, but once you have started, you will have a lifetime's supply. Turmeric can be planted between spring and fall outdoors or indoors in the early winter. You will need a large pot, at least 2 feet wide and 4 feet deep. Look for the little buds and plant a piece of turmeric 2 inches under the soil with the buds facing up.

Ginger can be grown the same way, but remember, it is very fussy when it comes to frost. Before planting a ginger rhizome, soak it in warm water overnight to speed up the initial growth.

You can grow a new head of garlic from one clove. Break a head of garlic up and pop a few cloves into the soil with the slimmest point facing upward. The cloves should be around 1 inch under the soil.

If you know someone with a plant you would like to use for herbal remedies, you can ask them for a cutting. Scan the stem of a plant to find a root node, a small new growth at a section of the stem that separates into a new stem. Cut the stem below the root node and pop the cutting in water, changing the water every few days. When the new roots reach 4 to 5 inches, you can plant the cutting in soil.

STEP 3 : MAKING SURE YOUR HERBS HAVE HEALTHY GROWTH

Watering should be simple, but it takes a little while to get the right balance between drowning plants and leaving them dehydrated. In the early stages and until the young plants get a little strength, use a mister to protect the spouts from the damaging force of a stream of water. The goal is to keep the soil moist. Once plants are established, you still want the topsoil to stay moist, but it's a good idea to water well every other day. Water passes deeper into the soil, and this encour- ages root growth.

Maintaining an herb garden is relatively simple if you have taken the time to correct your soil and create your own compost. Aside from water, your main task is to prune the plants. Pruning is like giving plants a haircut, and it keeps them healthy.

There are different techniques for pruning depending on the end goal. Deadheading means removing dead flower heads to encourage new flowers to bloom. Pinching is a method that removes the tops of plants to encourage more shoots to grow from each stem. It's called pinching because you usually use your fingertips to pinch the top of the plant. It's an excellent practice for herbs.

Some plants will also do well with a harder prune in spring or fall (not in the winter when they are dormant). Perennials, in particular, are plants that can be cut right back in the fall or spring, and they amazingly bloom back to life. This is a good way to keep the plant growing to the size and shape you want.

The general rule for pruning is to cut back no more than 25% of the foliage. Always cut just above the node where leaves meet the stem and cut at a 45-degree angle. This is the best way to prevent disease.

STEP 4: HARVESTING HERBS FOR MAXIMUM BENEFITS

One of the biggest advantages of having an herb garden is that you can access fresh flavors when you need them. In this sense, you can pinch a stem of a few leaves and add them straight to your dishes. When it comes to a larger harvest to create herbal remedies, the trick is to harvest plant parts when they have the highest amounts of flavor and health benefits.

You might be tempted to leave herbs until the end of summer for a larger harvest, but by then, the leaves are a little tired. Harvest your herbs in the summer just before they flower because the leaves will have the most flavor. If you are harvesting a plant for its flowers, the ideal time is when they just open before insects pollinate them. That being said, save some flowers for the bees! Lavender is an exception; stems should be harvested when two-thirds of the flowers are open. To harvest the seeds from flowers, pop the flower heads in a paper bag to dry, and once they are ready, shake the bag to dislodge the seeds.

Berries rich in antioxidants will have the most amount of antioxidants when they are ripe. The changing colors and the stronger aroma tell you when the fruit is ripe. They should be firm but not hard, and the easiest way is to taste one.

Harvesting roots can be trickier, but you have nothing to fear. Let's start with our favorites garlic, ginger, and turmeric. Garlic usually matures 7 to 8 months after plant- ing, whereas ginger and turmeric may take around ten months. A more accurate way to tell when the roots are ready is that the green foliage will start to die, turn brown, and dry out. Dig up the whole plant. Don't be tempted to pull on the dried stems because you risk damaging the roots. If you are growing in containers, tip the entire container upside down, and if not, use a trowel to move the soil away gently. Take what you need but don't forget to re-plant some of the rhizomes or garlic heads for the next season.

Perennial plants need more care. There is a little skill in carefully moving soil from around the base of the plant and choosing the best roots. You will notice a main cluster of roots, where they will be larger and denser. These need to stay in the ground so the plant will keep growing. Choose the roots that are growing around this central cluster. It will help if you add fresh soil with some compost to the area where you have harvested roots to ensure better growth.

The time of day is equally important. The best time of day is mid-morning. It will allow flowers to open, and the dew will have had time to evaporate.

STEP 5: WHICH STORAGE METHOD IS BEST?

For our pharmacy to last longer than just the growing season, it is essential to learn how to store herbs to maintain all their benefits and flavor. Even fresh herbs can be stored to make them last a little bit longer. The method goes back to whether they are hardy or tender herbs.

Once you have harvested your tender herbs, you can pop them in a mason jar with some water and keep them in the fridge for up to 2 weeks. Hardy herbs are wrapped in damp kitchen paper and popped in a sealed plastic bag in the fridge for about two weeks. The same preparation method can be used for hardy herbs, and then they can be frozen. Tender herbs can be wrapped similarly, but it's often more practical to make frozen herb cubes. Add the chopped tender herbs to an ice cube tray, and then add water, butter, or oil. When you need to use the herbs, pop one of the cubes into your recipe.

Basil is an exception. It doesn't do well in the fridge, so it is best to leave it in a mason jar with some water on the kitchen counter. If you want to freeze basil, you will need to blanche it first so that it keeps its color. Dip the leaves in boiling water for a few seconds and then freeze them.

For long-term storage, leaves, flowers, seeds, and roots must be dried. There are different methods, and while many rave about a dehydrator, it's unnecessary. You can dry plant parts in the oven on the lowest setting; just make sure all the parts are spread out well and not on top of each other. Ginger and turmeric can be sliced before drying. Microwaving is another, even faster, method. It will take a few minutes rather than hours, but you risk the heat destroying some active ingredients. Microwave for 30-second intervals and turn the parts each time.

Air drying is my favorite method. Tie your harvest into bundles and hang the bundles upside down. This way, all the essential oils flow into the leaves. It will take a few weeks for herbs to dry properly. Whichever method you choose, it is crucial that all parts are completely dry. Any moisture left in the plant parts could cause mold once stored in containers. Use a mortar and pestle or coffee grinder to turn dried parts into powders. Keep all your dried herbs and spices in sepa- rate air-tight containers and label your jars with what is in them and when you preserved them. Most will be good for up to 2 years.

To end our impressive information on herbs, I have created a simple chart that shows the general information at a glance. There are seven sections, those herbs that boost the immune system, help your skin, and may be effective against cancer, heart health, brain health, muscles and bones, and relaxation. To simplify things slightly, heart health includes diabetes; brain health includes headaches, migraines, and toothache; and relaxation includes anxiety and depression. Those with an asterisk can help with pregnancy, and although black cohosh isn't typically used for depression, it may improve symptoms of menopausal depression, so it is in this section.

Finally, those in bold are the herbs considered superfoods or some of the highest in antioxidants.

Chart 1

Herbal Information at a Glance

Plant	Immune System	Skin	Muscles and Bones	Cancer	Heart Health	Brain Health	Relax ation
Allspice				x			
Aloe vera		x	x		x	x	x
Amla		x					
Ashwagandha							x
Basil				x	x		
Black cohosh							x*
Black cumin				x			
Black elderberry	x						
Borage			x				
Brahmi							x
Burdock		x					
Butterbur	x						
Cilantro				x			
Caraway				x			
Cardamon				x			
Calendula		x					
Cat's Claw			x				
Cayenne			x		x		
Chamomile		x					x
Cinnamon				x	x		
Comfrey		x					

Coriander							x
Dandelion		x					
Dill				x			
Echinacea	x	x					
Eucalyptus			x				
Fenugreek					x		
Feverfew			x				
Garlic					x	x	
Ginger*	x		x		x	x	x
Ginkgo biloba		x					x
Ginseng			x		x	x	
Goldenseal	x						
Gotu kola		x				x	
Hawthorn					x		
Holy basil					x		x
Honeysuckle							x
Horseradish							x
Horsetail		x					
Kava kava							x
Lavender		x					x
Lemon balm*						x	x
Linden					x		
Marshmallow		x					
Milk thistle		x			x		
Moringa*						x	x
Motherwort					x		
Neem		x					
Oregano	x	x		x			
Parsley				x	x		
Passionflower							x

Peppermint*		x	x			x	x
Perilla	x						
Red clover			x				
Red sage			x				
Rose					x		
Rosemary		x	x			x	
Sage						x	
Sea buckthorn	x						
Stinging nettles	x	x					
St. John's wort		x					x
Thyme			x	x	x	x	x
Turmeric			x	x	x	x	x
Valerian							x
Yarrow							x

That's it! You have the extraction techniques, the plant bene- fits, and 5 simple steps to growing these incredible plants. As a little bonus, our final chapter will be recipes that will help you use up your patio potions, whether spicing up a meal or creating a special remedy.

FINAL REMINDER: *Have you •ownloa•e• your* ***full-color*** *reference gui•e to all the herbs we •iscuss in this book? When you rea• about an herb, it is helpful to see it an• know what we are talking about.*

Scan this bar code *Or go to*

referenceguide.homesteadmindset.com

Any •ifficulties? Email me •irectly at hello@homestea•min•set.com

menu:

21

SIMPLE RECIPES AND REMEDIES FOR YOU TO TRY

Have you ever noticed how children are more inclined to eat different things when they have cooked recipes themselves? The same thing happens when you grow your own herbs and spices. Suddenly, you will find yourself trying new recipes to use what you have grown yourself. Even those who aren't keen on cooking can start to have more fun. (I lump myself into this category!)

In this chapter, you will find some recipes that will hopefully give you more ideas for using your herbs, and we will look at ways you can create some remedies for different uses. But should you be using fresh or dried herbs?

IS FRESH ALWAYS BEST?

It's been drilled into our minds that fresh is best, and in many cases, this is true. For herbs, it's not always the case. Fresh herbs have higher amounts of vitamins, but as most of our focus has been on antioxidants, dried is best. The process of drying herbs completely slows down the degradation of antioxidants. The levels of antioxidants are measured in ORAC (Oxygen Radical Absorbance Capacity). Fresh parsley has 1,301 ORAC, which sounds good but is nothing compared to 73,670 ORAC when dried.

Rosemary is another amazing example. Fresh rosemary has 11,070 ORAC but dried, it is a whopping 165,280 ORAC (Superfoodly, 2020).

Your health will appreciate it if you try using fresh and dried herbs. Some herbs, like parsley, are best used fresh because they lose their flavor when dried. If you use dried herbs, add them at the beginning of cooking so they have time to work their magic. Add fresh herbs in the last 10 minutes of cook- ing. If you want to use fresh instead of dried or vice versa, use the ratio of 1 part dried equals 3 parts fresh.

I'm not very good with exact measurements, so feel free to add more or less of everything depending on your taste.

GARLIC AND PARSLEY CHICKEN

- chicken breast chopped
- 1 onion
- 4 cloves of garlic
- 1 cup of white wine
- ½ cup of cream or plain yogurt
- ½ cup of parmesan
- 1 teaspoon of dried parsley
- ½ teaspoon of basil
- ½ teaspoon of oregano
- a few sprigs of fresh parsley chopped

Heat a small amount of olive oil in a frying pan and fry the onions and chicken breast. Add the chopped garlic (make sure you have chopped it 10 minutes before adding it because it takes this long for the compounds such as allicin to develop). Once the chicken is cooked, add the wine and dried herbs. Leave it on a low heat for 10 to 15 minutes. Stir in the cream or yogurt and slowly add the parmesan, mixing, so there are no lumps. Add some salt and pepper along with the fresh parsley and leave it on low heat for 10 more minutes.

HERBY MEAT MARINADE

- ½ cup of cilantro
- ½ cup of basil
- ½ cup of rosemary
- ½ cup of thyme
- ½ cup of mint
- ½ cup oil
- ½ lemon juice
- 6 cloves of garlic
- 1 tablespoon of honey
- salt and pepper

Chop the garlic and finely chop the fresh herbs. Mix all the ingredients together in a bowl and add the meat. The great thing about this recipe is that the flavors work well with all meat and fish.

BLACK ELDERBERRY AND HAWTHORN JAM

- 2 generous cups of black elderberries
- 2 generous cups of hawthorn berries
- ½ cup of sugar
- 2 tablespoons of lemon juice

Wash the berries and cut them in half. Add them to a saucepan with the sugar and lemon juice and mash with a fork or potato masher. The good thing about hawthorn is that the berries contain pectin. This is an ingredient used to thicken jams, so you don't need to worry about adding it. The lemon juice will help with the thickening. Boil for about 20 minutes and then keep an eye on it as it thickens. Pour a little onto the back of a frozen tablespoon and wipe your finger down the middle. If the jam doesn't dribble, you have the right consistency.

STINGING NETTLE SALAD

- 2 bunches of stinging nettle leaves (boiled and left to cool)
- 1 cup of lemon balm
- ¼ cup of mint
- ¼ cup of oregano
- additional salad options of your choice (tomatoes, cucumber, peppers, etc.)

As you can imagine, chop and mix your salad ingredients. If you want to add extra zing and health, drizzle ginger-infused oil or vinegar over it.

GINGER AND CHAMOMILE SYRUP

- 1 ginger rhizome
- 2 cups of chamomile flowers
- 6 cups of water
- 1 cup of honey or sugar

Cut the ginger into smaller pieces, roughly the size of the top of your thumb. Place them in a saucepan with chamomile and water. Bring the water to boil and then let it simmer for 20 to 30 minutes. Strain the decoction and then start your syrup by adding one cup of decoction and one cup of honey to a smaller saucepan. On a low heat, stir the mixture until it thickens into a syrup.

MORINGA AND TURMERIC TINCTURE

- moringa leaves
- turmeric rhizomes
- black peppercorns gin

I haven't listed the quantities because it will depend on the size of your mason jar. Fill the jar up with equal amounts of moringa and turmeric and a couple of tablespoons of black peppercorns to help with the absorption. Top the jar up with gin and shake daily for a month.

MEDITERRANEAN HERB OIL INFUSION

- basil
- cilantro
- fenugreek
- mint
- oregano
- parsley
- sage
- thyme
- olive oil

Basically, you will make your own type of herbes de Provence with an equal amount of each of the above herbs. You should use dried herbs to prevent moisture from turning the oil bad. Fill a mason jar with your herbs and top with olive oil. An alternative is to use the same herbs with white wine vinegar instead of oil.

TURMERIC, GINGER, AND GARLIC VINEGAR INFUSION

- turmeric rhizomes
- ginger rhizomes
- garlic cloves
- black peppercorns
- white wine vinegar

Again, the amounts will depend on the size of your mason jar but aim for equal amounts of these roots and a couple of spoons of black peppercorns. The ginger can be cut into smaller pieces, and the garlic should be cut in half or quar- ters. You can use the same ingredients with olive oil instead of vinegar.

CALENDULA AND PEPPERMINT SALVE

- 1 cup of calendula flowers
- 1 cup of peppermint leaves
- 2 cups of coconut oil beeswax pellets

Add coconut oil, calendula flowers, and peppermint leaves in a double boiler (heatproof dish in a saucepan of water). Make sure all the plant parts are covered in oil. Heat the oil for 2 hours, just enough so it gently bubbles. Once cooled enough to handle, strain the oil and return one cup to the dish. Add 1 oz of beeswax pellets and mix while the wax melts. If you have a couple of *Aloe vera* leaves, now would be the time to scrape the gel and add it to the salve.

HOLY BASIL AND LEMON BALM COCKTAILS

holy basil and lemon balm tincture tonic
ice strawberries
holy basil and lemon balm leaves to decorate

I call this the healthiest possible way of having a bad moment! Get a lovely large glass and fill it with ice cubes and a few slices of strawberries. Add the tincture, making it as weak or strong as you like it. Top the glass up with a tonic and impress your friends with some fresh leaves for decoration.

I could go on for ages with different ideas for herbs and spices, but at the same time, I would love for this to be just enough to spike your interest and encourage you to explore. Take advantage of any leftovers to make extra herbal creations and pass them on to friends and family.

CONCLUSION

As we reach the end of this fascinating look at herbal remedies, I am blessed to be able to step into my garden every day and remind myself that there is no need to rely so heavily on pharmacies. There are so many other ways to spend our money rather than handing over profits to large pharmaceutical companies! The cost of practically every- thing is rising across countries worldwide, and our health is likely to suffer.

As budgets tighten, it won't be the luxury goods that we will miss. Organic food will be impossible as even the cost of non-organically produced goods is soaring. While our bodies lack the essential minerals and vitamins, stress levels and the risk of health problems and chronic diseases will continue to increase.

We could get wrapped up in the doom and gloom, or we can take our health into our own hands or, more specifically, into our gardens. It is just a case of 5 simple steps starting with getting to know your soil and ensuring that even before you plant any seed. If you are nervous about your soil condi- tions and the climate, pots and containers are an ideal solution.

Don't overwhelm yourself and plant too many things at once. There will be time to add elements, and once your first seeds have germinated, you will have more confidence for the next attempt. Take advantage of spring and fall for planting different things and bring some extra calm into your home by adding some herbs to your windowsills. Use a calendar to track what you plant, the best pruning and harvesting time, and remember to label all your herbal reme- dies with the ingredients and the date you made them.

With so many excellent choices, choosing just two or three plants to start your collection seems impossible. My best advice would be to grow something for your heart, some- thing for your brain, something for pain, and something for your skin. At least, this is a good starting point. The culinary herbs are the simplest to grow and are good for your confi- dence, as are chilies. Try always to choose organic seeds. They will likely be more expensive, but as you can make them last for years, it's worth it.

The main benefit of herbs is the incredible levels of antioxi- dants. They are becoming increasingly essential in our diets because of the lifestyles we lead. Some of these are our responsibility, like highly processed foods and insufficient exercise. Stress isn't our fault, but it is still another factor. Others are environmental such as pollution. These harmful influences create an imbalance between the body's natural antioxidants and free radicals, which can lead to chronic conditions, including diabetes, heart disease, cancer, and dementia.

Turmeric and ginger are two spices with some of the highest levels of antioxidants, and alma, cinnamon, and clove are top contenders too. When it comes to our culinary herbs, peppermint, oregano, rosemary, and thyme are fantastic. Because garlic is so easy to introduce into your diet, pop this one on your list too.

You don't have to wait for herbs and spices to grow in your garden. The next time you are at the store, pick up some key herbs and spices to kick-start your pharmacy. Be sure to choose organic garlic, ginger, and turmeric so that you can use some and plant some.

I genuinely hope that you have learned a tremendous amount from this book and that this has confirmed the evidence supporting the use of herbs.

Always combine this with your common sense. You will also have learned that there is immense power in these little plants, and they should be used respectfully and safely. Start with smaller doses orally and/or test patches topically in case of allergic reactions. Check with your doctors about interactions with your current medications, and if, for example, you are using a particular herb for insomnia, don't take it when you are about to get in your car. Common sense and safe usage should rule the day.

Creating herbal remedies with these basics in mind will ensure you are getting the most out of them but not putting yourself at risk. In just a short time, you will be experiencing the amazing gains nature has made for us and will start to see fewer trips to the pharmacy.

If you have enjoyed this book and are on your way to making some herbal remedies, I would love to hear how you are getting on. A quick review on Amazon would be a tremendous help for me to hear inspiring stories, but more importantly, other people can see just how easy it is to grow their own herbal remedies and take control of their health too. Thank you, and I wish you the best of luck!

And don't forget you can email me anytime at hello@home steadmindset. com.

Scan the QR code below for a quick review!

REFERENCES

Akhondzadeh, S. (2003, July). *Melissa officinalis extract in the treatment of patients with mil• to mo•erate Alzheimer's •isease: A •ouble blin•, ran•omise•, placebo-controlle• trial.* NIH. https://pubmed.ncbi.nlm.nih.gov/12810768/

Alkhatib, H. (2020, July 18). *Thymoquinone content in markete• black see• oil in*

Malaysia. NIH. https://www.ncbi.nlm.nih.gov/pmc/articles/ PMC7574749/

American Cancer Society. (n.d.). *Cancer facts & figures 2021.* Cancer Org. https://www.cancer.org/research/cancer-facts-statistics/all-cancer-facts- figures/cancer-facts-figures-2021.html

Asif, M. (2011, March 4). *Health effects of omega-3,6,9 fatty aci•s: Perilla frutescens is a goo• example of plant oils.* NIH. https://www.ncbi.nlm.nih. gov/pmc/articles/PMC3167467/

Barrett, B. (2010, December 21). *Echinacea for treating the common col•: A ran•omize• trial.* NIH. https://pubmed.ncbi.nlm.nih.gov/21173411/

Bhattacharyya, D. (2008, September). *Controlle• programme• trial of Ocimum sanctum leaf on generalize• anxiety •isor•ers.* NIH. https://pubmed.ncbi.nlm.nih.gov/19253862/

Bionic Products. (2016, May 27). *FDA Fin•s Majority of Herbal Supplements Don't Contain What They Claim.* Elanramedical. https://elanra.com/fda- finds-majority-of-herbal-supplements-dont-contain-what-they-claim/

Blau, J. N. (2004, January 6). *Water-•eprivation hea•ache: A new hea•ache with two variants.* American Headache Society. https://headachejournal.onlineli brary.wiley.com/doi/abs/10.1111/j.1526-4610.2004.04014.x

Bone, K. (2007, November). *Feverfew an• migraine hea•aches.* Gale Academic Onefile. https://go.gale.com/ps/i.do?id=GALE%7CA170509467&sid=googleScholar&v=2.1&it=r&linkaccess=abs&issn=&p=AONE&sw=w&userGroupName=anon%7E6543f25c

Bruce, D. F. (2013, February 13). *Cinnamon an• •iabetes.* WebMD. https:// www.webmd.com/diabetes/cinnamon-and-benefits-for-diabetes

Calabrese, C. (2008, July). *Effects of a stan•ar•ize• Bacopa monnieri extract on cognitive performance, anxiety, an• •epression in the el•erly: A ran•omize•, •ouble-blin•, placebo-controlle• trial.* NIH. https://www.ncbi.nlm.nih.gov/ pmc/articles/PMC3153866/

Centers for Disease Control and Prevention. (2021a, October 12). *The arthri- tis-mental health connection.* https://www.cdc.gov/arthritis/communica tions/features/arthritis-mental-health.htm

Centers for Disease Control and Prevention. (2021b, December 16). *What is •iabetes?*https://www.cdc.gov/diabetes/basics/diabetes.html

ChemDiv. (2017). *Worrie• about osteoporosis? Take turmeric! In•ian spice improves bone •ensity by up to 7%, stu•y reveal.* https://www.chemdiv.com/company/media/pharma-news/2017/worried-osteoporosis-take-turmeric-indian-spice-improves-bone-density-7-study-reveal/

Chen, W. (2019, December 9). *Review of ginseng anti-•iabetic stu•ies.* NIH. https://www.ncbi.nlm.nih.gov/pmc/articles/PMC6943541/

Chopin, M., & Littenberg, B. (2017, January 9). *The association of hot re• chili pepper consumption an• mortality: A large Population-Base• cohort stu•y.* NIH. https://www.ncbi.nlm.nih.gov/pmc/articles/PMC5222470/

Deal, C. L. (1991, June). *Treatment of arthritis with topical capsaicin: A •ouble- blin• trial.* NIH. https://pubmed.ncbi.nlm.nih.gov/1954640/

Diego, M. A. (1998, December). *Aromatherapy positively affects moo•, EEG patterns of alertness an• math computations.* NIH. https://pubmed.ncbi.nlm. nih.gov/10069621/

Eghdampour, F. (2013, November 30). *The impact of Aloe vera an• calen•ula on perineal healing after episiotomy in primiparous women: A ran•omize• clinical trial.* NIH. https://pubmed.ncbi.nlm.nih.gov/25276736/

Enkhtaivan, G. (2017, July 13). *Discovery of berberine base• •erivatives as anti-*

influenza agent through blocking of neuramini•ase. NIH. https://pubmed. ncbi.nlm. nih.gov/28958846/

Farooqui, A. A. (2018, May 15). *Ayurve•ic me•icine for the treatment of •ementia: Mechanistic aspects.* NIH. https://www.ncbi.nlm.nih.gov/pmc/articles/ PMC5976976/

Food for Breast Cancer. (2022, May 29). *Basil is recommen•e• for breast cancer in mo•eration.* https://foodforbreastcancer.com/foods/basil

Fortunato, P. (2020, January 24). *The struggle is real: Growing me•ication insecu- rities require new Rx strategies.* RxBenefits. https://www.rxbenefits.com/ blogs/ growing-medication-insecurities-require-new-rx-strategies/

Gopalakrishnan, L. (2016, June). *Moringa oleifera: A review on nutritive importance an• its me•icinal application.* ScienceDirect. http://www.sciencedirect. com/ science/article/pii/S2213453016300362,%20

Guo, Y. (2014, September 29). *Salvia miltiorrhiza: An ancient Chinese herbal me•icine as a source for anti-osteoporotic •rugs.* ScienceDirect. https://www. sciencedirect. com/science/article/abs/pii/S0378874114005777?via% 3Dihub

Hajimoosayi, F. (2020). *Effect of ginger on the bloo• glucose level of women with gestational •iabetes mellitus (GDM) with impaire• glucose tolerance test (GTT): A ran•omize• •ouble-blin• placebo-controlle• trial.* NIH. https://www.ncbi.nlm. nih.gov/pmc/articles/PMC7168816/

Hitti, M. (2008, February 26). *Curry spice may thwart heart failure.* WebMD.

https://www.webmd.com/heart-disease/heart-failure/news/20080226/ curry-spice-may-thwart-heart-failure

Jamshidi, N., & Cohen, M. (2017, March 16). *The clinical efficacy an• safety of tulsi in humans: A systematic review of the literature.* NIH. https://www.ncbi. nlm. nih.gov/pmc/articles/PMC5376420/

Janda, K. (2020, December 19). *Passiflora incarnata in neuropsychiatric •isor•ers*

—A systematic review. NIH. https://www.ncbi.nlm.nih.gov/pmc/articles/ PMC7766837/

Johanna, S. (2015, December 16). *How to use fenugreek see•s to treat •iabetes.* Medindia. https://www.medindia.net/news/healthinfocus/how-fenu greek-seeds-can-treat-diabetes-mellitus-156209-1.htm

Jun, Y. S. (2013, June 18). *Effect of eucalyptus oil inhalation on pain an• inflamma- tory responses after total knee replacement: A ran•omize• clinical trial.* NIH. https://www.ncbi.nlm.nih.gov/pmc/articles/PMC3703330/

Kamaleeswari, M., & Nalini, N. (2006, August). *Dose-response efficacy of caraway (Carum carvi L.) on tissue lipi• peroxi•ation an• antioxi•ant profile in rat colon carcinogenesis.* NIH. https://pubmed.ncbi.nlm.nih.gov/16872560/

Karbasforooshan, H. (2018, November 27). *Topical silymarin a•ministration for prevention of acute ra•io•ermatitis in breast cancer patients: A ran•omize•, •ouble-blin•, placebo-controlle• clinical trial.* NIH. https://pubmed.ncbi.nlm. nih.gov/30479044/

Kasmaei, H. D. (2016, January 2). *Effects of Corian•rum sativum syrup on migraine: A ran•omize•, Triple-Blin•, Placebo-Controlle• trial.* NIH. https:// pubmed.ncbi.nlm.nih.gov/26889386/

Khalsa, K. P. S., DN-C. RH. (2021, May 19). *Top 3 herbs for heart health.* Better Nutrition. https://www.betternutrition.com/conditions-and-wellness/heart-health/herbs-for-heart-health/

Kim, H. (2018, October). *Panax ginseng as an a•juvant treatment for Alzheimer's •isease.* ScienceDirect. https://www.sciencedirect.com/science/article/pii/S1226845317303524

Korea University. (2016, May 20). *Sweet flavor of ginger can serve as a natural ingre•ient that prevents tooth •ecay.* Korea AC. https://www.korea.ac.kr/ user/boardList.do?boardId=366&siteId=en&page=1&id= en_060101000000&boardSeq=470280&command=albumView

Koulivand, P. H. (2013, March 14). *Laven•er an• the nervous system.* NIH. https://www.ncbi.nlm.nih.gov/pmc/articles/PMC3612440/

Kumar, V. S., & Navaratnam, V. (2013, July 3). *Neem (Aza•irachta in•ica): Prehistory to contemporary me•icinal uses to humankin•.* NIH. https://www. ncbi.nlm.nih.gov/pmc/articles/PMC3695574/

Kwon, H. (2010, July 24). *Cinnamon extract in•uces tumor cell •eath through inhibition of NFκB an• AP1.* NIH. https://www.ncbi.nlm.nih.gov/pmc/articles/PMC2920880/

Lee, S. (2010, March 3). *Effect of German chamomile oil application on alleviating atopic •ermatitis-like immune alterations in mice.* NIH. https://www.ncbi. nlm.nih.gov/pmc/articles/PMC2833428/

Maenthaisong, R. (2006, September). *The efficacy of aloe vera use• for burn woun• healing: A systematic review.* ScienceDirect. https://www.sciencedi rect.com/science/article/abs/pii/S0305417906007029

Mancuso, M. (2020, June 1). *The antibacterial activity of Mentha.* Interchopen. https://www.intechopen.com/chapters/72371

Mansoui, P. (2017, December). *The impact of topical Saint John's wort (Hypericum perforatum) treatment on tissue tumor necrosis factor-alpha levels in plaque-type psoriasis: A pilot stu•y.* NIH. https://www.ncbi.nlm.nih.gov/pmc/articles/PMC5664864/

Montes, P. (2015). *Ginkgo biloba extract 761: A review of basic stu•ies an• potential clinical use in psychiatric •isor•ers.* NIH. https://pubmed.ncbi.nlm.nih.gov/25642989/

Moringa Facts. (2017, May 30). *Moringa benefits for breastfee•ing mothers.* Moringa Facts. https://moringafacts.net/tag/mothers/

Moscow Institute of Physics and Technology. (2016, June 28). *Compoun•s in parsley an• •ill help fight cancer, research shows.* ScienceDaily. https://www.sciencedaily.com/releases/2016/06/160628114610.htm

Movafegh, A. (2008, June). *Preoperative oral Passiflora incarnata re•uces anxiety in ambulatory surgery patients: A •ouble-blin•, placebo-controlle• stu•y.* NIH. https://pubmed.ncbi.nlm.nih.gov/18499602/

Mur, E. (2002, April). *Ran•omize• •ouble-blin• trial of an extract from the penta- cyclic alkaloi•-chemotype of uncaria tomentosa for the treatment of rheumatoi• arthritis.* NIH. https://pubmed.ncbi.nlm.nih.gov/11950006/

Oliver, J. M. (2016, August 17). *Novel form of curcumin improves en•othelial function in young, healthy in•ivi•uals: A •ouble-blin• placebo controlle• stu•y.* Hindawi. https://www.hindawi.com/journals/jnme/2016/1089653/

Pan, S. (2014, April 27). *Historical perspective of tra•itional in•igenous me•ical practices: The current renaissance an• conservation of herbal resources.* NIH. https://www.ncbi.nlm.nih.gov/pmc/articles/PMC4020364/

Panahi, Y. (2015, February). *Rosemary oil vs minoxi•il 2% for the treatment of an•rogenetic alopecia: A ran•omize• comparative trial.* NIH. https://pubmed.ncbi.nlm.nih.gov/25842469/

Pfizer. (n.d.). *How the immune system protects you from infection.* https://www. pfizer. com/news/articles/ how_the_immune_system_protects_you_from_infection

Pittler, M. H., MD. (2003, June 1). *Hawthorn extract for treating chronic heart failure: Meta-analysis of ran•omize• trials.* ScienceDirect. https://www. sciencedirect. com/science/article/abs/pii/S0002934303001311

PubChem. (n.d.). *Morphine.* NIH. https://pubchem.ncbi.nlm.nih.gov/ compound/ Morphine

Qorbanpour, M. (2018, August 14). *Effect of •ietary ginger (Zingiber officinale roscoe) an• multi-strain probiotic on growth an• carcass traits, bloo• biochem- istry, immune responses an• intestinal microflora in broiler chickens.* NIH. https:// pubmed.ncbi.nlm.nih.gov/30011890/

Raghif, A. A. (2015, October). *A comparative stu•y of the effect of thyme an• calcium with vitamin D3 in treatment of postmenopausal women with osteo- porosis.* ResearchGate. https://www.researchgate.net/publication/ 282506206_A_Comparative_Study_of_the_Effect_of_Thyme_and_Calci um_with_Vitamin_D3_in_Treatment_of_postmenopausal_Women_with_ Osteoporosis

Ramchandani, S. (2020, December 28). *An overview of the potential anticancer properties of car•amonin.* Open Exploration. https://www.explorationpub. com/Journals/etat/Article/100226#:%7E:text=Moreover%2C%20carda monin%20was%20found%20to,arrest%20%5B70%E2%80%9371%5D

Rawson, C. (2021, March). *Milk thistle re•uces elevate• glucose.* LifeExtension. https:// www.lifeextension.com/magazine/2021/4/milk-thistle-reduces- glucose

Reza, P. (2005, January). *The effect of German chamomile mouthwash on •ental plaque an• gingival inflammation.* ResearchGate. https://www.researchgate. net/ publication/ 26619262_The_Effect_of_German_Chamomile_Mouthwash_ on_Den tal_Plaque_and_Gingival_Inflammation

Rezaee, M. (2019, September 29). *The effect of essential oil of rosemary on eccen- tric exercise-in•uce• •elaye•-onset muscle soreness in non-active women.* Wageningen Academic Publishers. https://www.wageningenacademic. com/doi/10.3920/ CEP190034

Rezaei, M. (2015, April). *Evaluation of the antibacterial activity of the Althaea officinalis L. leaf extract an• its woun• healing potency in the rat mo•el of exci- sion woun• creation.* NIH. https://www.ncbi.nlm.nih.gov/pmc/articles/ PMC4418059/

Ried, K. (2016, January 27). *The effect of age• garlic extract on bloo• pressure an•*

other car•iovascular risk factors in uncontrolle• hypertensives: The AGE at heart trial. NIH. https://www.ncbi.nlm.nih.gov/pmc/articles/PMC4734812/

Salve, J. (2019, December). *A•aptogenic an• anxiolytic effects of ashwagan•ha root*

extract in healthy a•ults: A •ouble-blin•, ran•omize•, placebo-controlle• clinical stu•y. NIH. https://www.ncbi.nlm.nih.gov/pmc/articles/PMC6979308/

Sarris, J. (2011, January 1). *Kava: A comprehensive review of efficacy, safety, an•*

psychopharmacology. Sage Journals. https://journals.sagepub.com/doi/10.3109/00048674.2010.522554

Schapowal, A. (2002, January 19). *Ran•omise• controlle• trial of butterbur an• cetirizine for treating seasonal allergic rhinitis.* The BMJ. https://www.bmj.com/content/324/7330/144

Shamaladevi, N. (2013, April 8). *Ericifolin: a novel antitumor compoun• from allspice that silences an•rogen receptor in prostate cancer.* OUP Academic. https://academic.oup.com/carcin/article/34/8/1822/2463180?login= false

Shikov, A. N. (2011, April). *Effect of Leonurus car•iaca oil extract in patients with arterial hypertension accompanie• by anxiety an• sleep •isor•ers.* NIH. https://pubmed.ncbi.nlm.nih.gov/20839214/v

Shishehbor, F. (2018, May 3). *Cinnamon consumption improves clinical symptoms an• inflammatory markers in women with rheumatoi• arthritis.* Taylor & Fran- cis. https://www.tandfonline.com/doi/full/10.1080/07315724.2018. 1460733

Shoba, G. (1998, May). *Influence of piperine on the pharmacokinetics of curcumin in animals an• human volunteers.* NIH. https://pubmed.ncbi.nlm.nih.gov/9619120/

Spraul, T. (2020, August 25). *How much •oes the average American spen• on supplements?* Exercise.Com. https://www.exercise.com/learn/how-much- does-the-average-american-spend-on-supplements/

Summer, J. (2022, March 11). *Valerian root for sleep.* Sleep Foundation. https://www.sleepfoundation.org/sleep-aids/valerian-root

Superfoodly. (2020, June 8). *Fresh vs. •rie• herbs: What's healthier? Not what you think.* Superfoodly |. https://www.superfoodly.com/fresh-vs-dried-herbs/ Sutalangka, C. (2013, December 23). *Moringa oleifera mitigates memory impairment an• neuro•egeneration in animal mo•el of age-relate• •ementia.* NIH.

https://www.ncbi.nlm.nih.gov/pmc/articles/PMC3884855/

Tang, E. L. H. (2013, December 9). *Antioxi•ant activity of Corian•rum sativum an• protection against DNA •amage an• cancer cell migration.* NIH. https:// www.ncbi.nlm.nih.gov/pmc/articles/PMC4028854/

The Silver Book. (2006). *Chronic •isease.* Silver Book. https://www.silverbook.org/condition/chronic-disease/

The University of Texas at El Paso. (n.d.). *Herbs to avoi• •uring pregnancy.* UTEP. https://www.utep.edu/herbal-safety/populations/herbs-to-avoid- during-pregnancy.html

Thorup, A. C. (2015, July 21). *Intake of novel re• clover supplementation for 12 weeks improves bone status in healthy menopausal women.* Hindawi. https:// www.hindawi.com/journals/ecam/2015/689138/

Times of India. (2021, December 6). *People who shoul• not have amla (gooseberry).* Times of India. https://timesofindia.indiatimes.com/life- style/health-fitness/health-news/people-who-should-not-have-amla- gooseberry/photostory/88122756.cms

University Of Newcastle Upon Tyne. (2009, September 1). *Sage improves memory, stu•y shows.* ScienceDaily. https://www.sciencedaily.com/releases/2003/09/030901091846.htm

Vijayan, N. A. (2012, February 15). *Anti-inflammatory an• anti-apoptotic effects of Crataegus oxyacantha on isoproterenol-in•uce• myocar•ial •amage.* NIH. https://pubmed.ncbi.nlm.nih.gov/22350754/

Wang, Y. (2016, June 3). *Evaluation of •aily ginger consumption for the prevention of chronic •iseases in a•ults: A cross-sectional stu•y.* NIH. https://pubmed. ncbi.nlm.nih.gov/28336112/

Warner, J. (2010, September 20). *Ginger may soothe aching muscles.* WebMD. https://www.webmd.com/pain-management/news/20100920/ginger- may-soothe-aching-muscles

WebMD Editorial Contributors. (2020, October 22). *Oregano oil: Is it goo• for you?* WebMD. https://www.webmd.com/diet/oregano-oil-good-for-you WHO. (2021, September 2). *Dementia.* https://www.who.int/news-room/fact-sheets/detail/dementia

Yongchaiyudha, S. (1996, November). *Anti•iabetic activity of Aloe vera L. juice. I. clinical trial in new cases of •iabetes mellitus.* NIH. https://pubmed.ncbi.nlm.nih.gov/23195077/

Zhai, Z. (2009, June 16). *Alcohol extract of Echinacea palli•a reverses stress- •elaye• woun• healing in mice.* NIH. https://www.ncbi.nlm.nih.gov/pmc/ articles/PMC2763438/

Zhang, D. (2013, November 24). *Curcumin an• •iabetes: Systematic review.* NIH. https://www.ncbi.nlm.nih.gov/pmc/articles/PMC3857752/